BRITISH BUTCHERS AND BUNGLERS OF WORLD WAR ONE

BRITISH BUTCHERS AND BUNGLERS OF WORLD WAR ONE

JOHN LAFFIN

Bramley
Books

A Sutton Publishing Book

This edition published in 1998 by Bramley Books
An imprint of Quadrillion Publishing Limited
Godalming Business Centre, Woolsack Way,
Godalming, Surrey GU7 1XW

ISBN 1-84100-012-4

This book was designed and produced by
Sutton Publishing Limited
Phoenix Mill · Thrupp · Stroud · Gloucestershire GL5 2BU

Typesetting and origination by
Sutton Publishing Limited
Printed in Great Britain by
WBC Limited, Bridgend, Mid-Glamorgan.

For the families of the soldiers killed, wounded or mentally damaged while serving under British military leadership during the 'Great War for Civilisation', 1914–18.

'I don't know what the brains of our officers are like, but the hearts of our men are beautiful and wonderful'
John Masefield, 15 March 1917,
in a letter to his wife
from the Somme battlefield.

CONTENTS

CONTENTS

ACKNOWLEDGEMENTS

As always, it is to Hazelle that I owe most in writing this book. She accompanies me on my explorations over all the battlefields described herein, encouraged me during the preparation and worked tirelessly on the typescript. Most importantly, she shares my conviction that a great wrong was committed against the British Commonwealth soldiers by many of their senior commanders.

I am grateful to the following publishers for permission to quote from certain books: Methuen & Co, *Great Britain and the War of 1914–1918*, by Llewellyn Woodward; Cassell Ltd., *History of the First World War*, by B.H. Liddell-Hart; Oxford University Press, *The Great War and Modern Memory*, by Paul Fussell; Picardy, *Poor Bloody Infantry*, by Archie Groom; Eyre & Spottiswoode, *The Private Papers of Douglas Haig*, edited by Robert Blake; Unwin Hyman, *Military Effectiveness: The First War*, by Paul Kennedy; Jonathan Cape, *On the Psychology of Military Incompetence*, by Norman F. Dixon. Also, Tim Travers, for permission to quote from his *The Killing Ground*.

The battlefield photographs come either from the Imperial War Museum, London, or the Australian War Memorial, Canberra, custodians of their national photographic collections.

Special thanks to my friend Martin Gilbert for permission to use the maps entitled 'Passchendaele – The Mud' and 'Trenches on the Western Front 1917'. Maps of the Western Front and the Somme come from my book *Brassey's Battles: 3,500 Years of Conflict, Campaigns and Wars from A–Z*. My thanks to Brassey's Defence Publishers.

John Laffin

PERSISTENT, TROUBLING QUESTIONS

'Hump your pack and get a move on. The next hour, man, will bring you three miles nearer your death. Your life and your death are nothing in these fields – nothing, no more than it is to the man planning the next attack at GHQ. You are not even a pawn.'

Guy Chapman, in a valediction
to an anonymous infantryman,
The Passionate Prodigality.

This book is the result of a lifelong study of war in general and the Great War of 1914–18 in particular. I make this point to emphasise that my opinions about the leadership of that war are not fired off in a spontaneous flash of anger, which many first-time visitors to World War I battlefields experience when they see – and are' horrified by – the great military cemeteries. Anger I have, and in depth, but it flows from long consideration.

I had a flying start in my study of the Great War because both my parents were directly involved in it. My father began the war as a member of the Australian Army Medical Corps and was later commissioned into the infantry. He served in Egypt, in the Gallipoli campaign and in France. My mother, as a sister in the Australian Army Nursing Service, served in Egypt, on Lemnos

Island – the base for Gallipoli – in France and England.

Together, my parents were a rich source of information. They also had interesting opinions, though even as a boy I did not simply take these as my own but as reference points from which to explore. After the war in civilian life my parents' friends were former soldiers and nursing sisters and I was born into this society of veterans. More information, more opinions and criticisms. A favourite uncle of mine had lost an entire arm in the fierce fighting at Morlancourt in 1918 and he, like the others, was a rich source of anecdote. I never heard him complain about his handicap but in this he was not unusual among wounded veterans.

Soldiers wounded in the Great War seemed to complain less than those hurt in the war of 1939–45. Most of them were, in a strange way, glad of a wound serious enough to take them out of the war. Since they had seen so many of their mates killed, often in horrible ways, their attitude was understandable.

Growing up in Australia, I excitedly watched the annual Anzac Day march in Sydney on 25 April, the date of the landing at Gallipoli in 1915. It was a tremendous spectacle – still is – and it outdoes in sentiment and emotion any comparable event in the world, except perhaps Bastille Day in France. My mother would not attend the marches because she had too many painful memories of men she had nursed but who had not survived to take part in the commemorative marches. She told me that she was still angry and bitter at the 'wicked waste of good men'. She was to remain angry and bitter until the end of her life at the age of ninety-two. Because she would not attend reunions, groups of her former patients and hospital orderlies came to our home on Anzac Day to pay their respects to my mother, whom they called 'Little Sister', because of her diminutive size.

Throughout the 1920s and '30s the Great War was one of my main reading interests. In 1940, when I lied about my age so as to qualify for enlistment in the second Australian Imperial Force (AIF), I came into contact with the very men about whom I had been reading, those of the first AIF.

They had enlisted for a second war and some actually managed to go abroad on active service. The greater number, being considered too old for service overseas, became instructors. They included a good number of former English, Welsh, Scottish and Irish ex-soldiers who had emigrated to Australia following the first war.

It did not take much effort to stimulate them into discussion of that earlier war. Many of them, more than 20 years later, had not yet recovered from the trauma of the trenches. In 1940 the British and Commonwealth armies were still using the weapons of the earlier war, notably the .303 Lee Enfield rifle, the Lewis light machine-gun and the No. 36 H.E. grenade (the Mills bomb). The veterans had not forgotten their experience with these arms, and the tactics which their use dictated, and we new soldiers learnt much from them.

Much of the training during the first years of World War II was based on lessons learnt during the fighting on the Western Front in 1918. Undergoing courses of instruction at various army schools, I heard innumerable lectures and took part in many exercises based on section, platoon, company and battalion tactics which had been evolved in France and Belgium a generation earlier.

Following service during World War II, I came back to the study of World War I. Because of my own military experience, I was now even more acutely aware of the differences in senior leadership between one war and the other. Even more than in the exercise of leadership, there seemed to be differences in *attitudes* to leadership.

Most senior generals of World War I were limited in their professionalism, in that they gave orders but when things went wrong they did not accept responsibility. Throughout the war it was common for them to blame failures on men who could not answer back – the dead, and the junior in rank. Also, failure was often attributed to 'bad luck' or the 'troops' inexperience'. If failure was the result of the troops' inexperience, as the generals said, then why did they send them into the bloodbath again and again? Were they hoping that after a few months the few survivors would have had so much experience that they could at last defeat the enemy? It made no logic to blame the men's inexperience and then to keep pushing them into the fire.

In World War II the senior generals had a wide-ranging professionalism, they followed through on their orders and they accepted the responsibility. Not that they had much option about this – generals who were considered to have failed were removed from command. In World War I some junior generals were relieved of command, sometimes because they were too obviously competent, therefore producing in their seniors feelings of inferiority and resentment. General French's political superiors withdrew him from command of the British Expeditionary Force, though only after several costly military failures over which he presided.

Again, the generals of World War I did sometimes have strategies, but possessed little apparent ability to put any strategy into effect. Those of World War II were more able both strategically and tactically.

Comparisons and contrasts between the two world wars are not only inevitable but essential because both were 'great' wars in scale and complexity. One startling contrast is that while World War II was fought in many more theatres and over six years, rather than four, the British Commonwealth's casualties were far fewer than in the earlier war, in fact 75 per cent fewer if we omit as casualties those soldiers taken prisoner. To what extent does this disparity indicate better leadership?

In my efforts to understand more about strategic and tactical decisions in World War I, I have visited, over and again, the old battlefields of Ypres Salient and the Somme, of Loos, Neuve Chapelle, Verdun, Chemin des Dames, Arras and Vimy, of Gallipoli and Palestine. As a boy I had known the casualty figures of the war, overall and battle by battle. Those which were most firmly fixed in my mind concerned the first day of the Battle of the Somme, 1 July 1916, when the British Army had 20,000 men killed and another 40,000 wounded. Knowing a statistic and being aware of its meaning on the ground are two different things, for on the ground are hundreds of cemeteries and scores of memorials.

PERSISTENT, TROUBLING QUESTIONS

On the great British memorial at Thiepval, the Somme, are recorded the names of 73,000 soldiers classified as missing. Another 55,000 names of the missing are engraved on the Menin Gate, Ypres. On several other memorials are smaller numbers of missing men. They are missing because their remains were never found. Often, nothing of them remained to be found. Tens of thousands of soldiers were blown to pieces or to a mulch of blood and bone by high explosive shells. The mud swallowed up others, sometimes while they were still alive.

Over a period of 35 years I have tramped thousands of miles over these battlefields, and not just in the most comfortable season. On the Western Front I have slogged through mud and driving rain in winter and at Gallipoli I have climbed the fearsome ridges in the stifling summer heat. There are two significant differences between my experiences and those of the men of the Great War. I could leave the field whenever I wished – and nobody was firing bullets and shells at me.

I have studied millions of words in memoirs, official histories and reports and despatches concerning the war. Much of this labour has been directly concerned with writing a particular book, but on a more long term basis I have sought the answers to persistently troubling questions. These are the main ones:

How could the Allied armies lose so many men and over such a long period without any significant gain in ground?

Why didn't the general public – as well as the press and pulpit – complain about the massive casualties?

Why did the generals persist, in one battle after another, with methods of attack long after they had been proved ineffective?

Similarly, when it was obvious that a particular attack had failed, and when heavy casualties then precluded success, why was it still pushed?

How could generals accept such calamitous losses on their own side with apparent equanimity?

Why was a general who was the architect of an offensive which caused the loss of 20,000 men on the first day permitted to remain in command of his battered army?

How were the senior generals able to conceal their inadequacies for so long?

Did no other strategies and other tactics exist?

Did the senior generals and their staffs have any conception of what they were asking their fighting soldiers to do? That is, did they know and understand about the conditions on the battlefield?

Why were independent commands – as at Gallipoli and in Mesopotamia – given to generals obviously too old, too unfit or otherwise unsuitable for the task?

Did any of the men in great authority have any sense of shame or remorse over their failures and the loss of life which ensued?

In finding answers to these questions I have concluded that some British generals were bunglers and butchers. The two went together because, under the conditions of warfare, butchery was the result of bungling. I am referring not to the butchering of enemy soldiers – this is the legitimate if deplorable business of war – but to the wholesale slaughter of British and Empire troops. In World War II it was possible for a communique to state, truthfully, that 'Our casualties were slight'. In the Great War casualties were always heavy but generals frequently reported them as light or 'relatively light'. Relative to what, they never explained.

The more senior the rank, the greater the influence and authority – and much greater the responsibility. But it goes further than this. The more senior the rank the more the opportunities for reward and honours and, conversely, the greater the responsibility for failure. At least, this is how matters should logically be ordered. In the Great War such logic was swept away and those men who had bungled most grievously received the highest awards and rewards.

A.J.P. Taylor[1] comments that 'those British generals who prolonged the slaughter kept their posts and won promotion.' I use the term slaughter as I think Taylor does, with the deliberate connotation that the generals concerned were all too ready to accept heavy casualties, that they had little or no sensitivity about the conditions under which their men lived and fought, and little or no remorse for the vast numbers of casualties which their campaigns and battles brought about.

Another writer who uses the word slaughter is a 'common soldier' – Private Arthur Russell[2] of the Machine-Gun Corps. He says, 'The hapless British soldiers were sent to their crucifixion and ultimate slaughter in the flooded marshlands of Flanders, owing to the simple fact that those responsible had little idea as to the impossible conditions which existed to enable any attacking movement to succeed on any large scale.'

Stephen Graham, a Guards private, wrote of the casualties:

> I do not know why the various occasions on which battalions have fought till there were merely a few score survivors have not been properly chronicled. . . . Certain platoons or companies fought shoulder to shoulder till the last man dropped or were shelled to nothingness, or getting over the top went forward till they all withered away under machine-gun fire. A fortnight after some exploit, a field marshal or divisional general comes down to a battalion to thank it for its gallant conduct, and fancies for a moment, perchance, that he is looking at the men who did the deed of valour, and not at a large draft that has just been brought up from England and the base to fill the gap. He should ask the services of the chaplain and make his congratulations in the grave-yard or go to the hospital and make them there.

In 1939 General Sir Archibald Wavell gave a series of lectures at Cambridge which became well-known in military and academic circles. He believed, he said, in the individual use of the infantryman. He meant that soldiers should be led resourcefully and cleverly, with tactics varying according to the conditions. To move men into battle in long waves as Haig had done, said Wavell, was to sanction mass butchery.

Norman Dixon[3] comments that 'Only the most blinkered could deny that the First World War exemplified every aspect of high-level military incompetence. For sheer lack of imaginative leadership, inept decisions, ignoring the military intelligence, under-estimation of the enemy, delusional optimism and monumental wastage of human resources it has surely never had its equal.'

The German Chief of General Staff, Field Marshal Erich Ludenorff, understood the failings of British military leaders. They pursued strategical aims without regard for the tactical difficulties, he said in his memoirs. The truth of this sharp professional criticism can be seen over and again in actions wherever the British fought, with the exception of Sinai and Palestine where the strategy was viable and the tactics were practical.

The commanders whom I consider to be the principal butchers and bunglers are presented here alphabetically. How they might be assessed on a table of fault and default may become apparent.

They are (with final ranks):

Field Marshal Lord French
General Sir Hubert Gough
Field Marshal Earl Haig
General Sir Richard Haking
General Sir Ian Hamilton
Lieut.-General Sir G.M. Harper
Lieut.-General Sir Aylmer Hunter-Weston
Field Marshal Lord Rawlinson
Lieut.-General Sir Frederick Stopford
Major-General Sir C.V. Townshend

Haig and his contemporaries had all studied the doctrines of the great nineteenth century Prussian military thinker Karl von Clausewitz. There was no possibility that they had *not* studied him because his work was required reading at both Sandhurst and the Staff College. Clausewitz argued that the defensive was stronger than the offensive. Nevertheless, Haig and others insisted that only the offensive could lead to decisive results, even though the defensive had become ever stronger since Clausewitz's time.

Haig had a clear mental idea – or more, an ideal – of what

'normal' war should be and how it should be fought. It should take place according to structured rules which had only to be followed for success to take place. Even before the war or a campaign began it was essential, in Haig's ideal, that the Commander-in-Chief should not allow himself to be distracted by diversions. Anything which took his attention away from the enemy's main force was a diversion. For Haig, the campaigns in Italy, Salonika, Gallipoli and Mesopotamia were diversions.

The assault against the main enemy army was made to the formula of manoeuvre, preparation, attack, exploitation, though manoeuvre may not always have been essential. During the preparatory stage the advanced guard – which might be a large part of the attacking forces – scouted, protected the main force, pinned down the enemy, deceived, engaged and wore him down. With all this achieved, the attackers' general reserve was then thrown in. Success was certain.

Right through to the end of 1916 senior officers and their staff regarded warfare as more predictable and simplified than it actually was. Few British commanders tried to grasp the nature of modern war and the alarming problems which it produced. This failure to understand would not have been so critical had the commanders conceded, even if only to themselves, that problems *existed*. Brigadier-General Rees was one who was blind to problems. He commanded 94th Infantry Brigade of the 31st Division and immediately after his brigade's advance on 1 July 1916 he wrote:

> They advanced in line after line, dressed as if on parade, and not a man shirked going through the extremely heavy barrage, or facing the machine-gun and rifle fire that finally wiped them out. I saw the lines which advanced in such admirable order melting away under the fire. Yet not a man wavered, broke the ranks, or attempted to come back. I have never seen, I would never have imagined, such a magnificent display of gallantry, discipline and determination. The reports I have had from the very few survivors of this marvellous advance bear out what I saw with my own eyes, viz, that hardly a man of ours got to the German front line.

This is an incredible report. Rees writes as if he had had a victory, yet the 'marvellous advance' failed and his men were virtually wiped-out. Mentally, he seems to have convinced himself that the gallantry, discipline and determination were the equivalent of victory. Perhaps an officer who had lost his entire command had to rationalise defeat in the way Rees did. More likely he was repeating the principle pushed by his seniors – that the offensive always triumphed. The 94th Brigade had been offensive, ergo it had triumphed.

Senior officers' approach to war was not only unintelligent, it was actively anti-intellectual. They were aware that fire-power had increased tremendously but did not apply their brains to methods of making progress against it. The phrase 'the offensive' was uttered as if, in itself, it was a solution. In fact, the generals developed 'the offensive' into a pseudo-doctrine of 'the offensive at all costs'. This was deemed to be the way to cope with the new fire-power – push more and more men at it. The enemy guns could not wipe out all of them and enough would surely get through to capture the enemy positions. This unofficial but widely held doctrine took on a corollary – that a sufficiently large mass of troops would always succeed eventually in an attack.

Haig and most of the generals of the time considered war to be a regulated and organised activity. For them it naturally fitted the schedules and plans they had drawn up. A battle, which they still often referred to by the old-fashioned label of 'an engagement', should be structured in the traditional Napoleonic manner of three or four stages. When confusion occurred the generals' first thought was to try to force order onto the battlefield. Haig persisted in his attempts to restore order and his simplistic method was to thrust more and more men forward as if by doing so he could soak up the confusion.

French, Haig, Rawlinson, Gough and many other generals seemed to believe that good organisation would win battles. It was only necessary to have infantry and artillery in their 'correct' places at the time of the assault and all would go well. In fact, success on 1 July 1916 really depended on the correct use of tactics for infantry and artillery, but such tactics were not used.

The manual, *Infantry Training* (1914) declared that 'Machine-guns are essentially weapons of opportunity.' British tactics certainly gave the German gunners every opportunity to employ them.

Even in March 1916, after 20 months of war in which the British had been cut to pieces by machine-guns, Haig wanted fewer of them in infantry battalions. Too many machine-guns, he judged, would make his soldiers defensive-minded and destroy the attack-at-all-costs principle. The higher commanders constantly demanded that their infantry achieve tasks beyond their powers, despite some brilliant achievements.

The British generals could see that battles would be murderous, but they reasoned that victory would certainly go to those who showed the greatest staunchness. Weapons were not the major factor, but will-power. Haig had pronounced this in 1907, in his *Cavalry Studies*. 'Success in battle depends mainly on moral [sic] and a determination to conquer.' Yet it was obvious that machine-guns and rifles used from static positions gave the advantage to the defender. The British had used Maxim machine-guns at Omdurman and inflicted great slaughter among the Dervishes. The Boer War of 1899–1902 had shown that brave British bayonet charges by men in line were futile, even against men armed with nothing more than rifles.

Some British generals may have understood all this but their careers depended on agreeing with their seniors that 'the charge is the thing'. Then, as the attacking troops came across the open ground the defenders would gradually panic and then run. It was as if the generals believed that nothing happened between the time the British troops left their trenches and arrived in those of the enemy. It is the only way in which their lunatic charges can be explained.

The *Cavalry Training Manual* of 1907 was quite explicit: 'It must be accepted as a principle that the rifle, effective as it is, cannot replace the effect produced by the speed of the horse, the magnetism of the charge and the terror of cold steel.'

In seeking to understand the unworkable tactics of the senior commanders – especially Haig, French and Gough – it must always be remembered that they were cavalry officers. This fact, and what followed from it, cannot be overstressed. They had no idea what it was like to be an infantryman, loaded with 66lb. of equipment and struggling over broken ground or through mud to do battle with the enemy. They seemed to think that men on foot could move as rapidly as men on horses – though perhaps they assumed this rather than thought about it. Real thought was conspicuously absent.

British generals were obsessed with attack. One official text-book comments that 'the most soldierly way out of what looks like an impossible situation is by attack. The moral effect is enormous.' Infantry Regulations emphasised the same point. 'The main essential to success is to close with the enemy, cost what it may. A determined and steady advance lowers the fighting spirit of the enemy.' Throughout the Boer War British soldiers had made determined and steady attacks but did nothing to lower the fighting spirit of the outnumbered Boers, who cut down the British in rows.

Hundreds of officers reached the rank of major-general and commanded a single division of up to 20,000 men. The great majority are 'unknown' in military history. They could not influence strategy and their tactics in a divisional operation were often imposed upon them by Corps and Army commanders. Some major-generals were interested in the welfare of their men and at least 30 were killed on active service. I have singled out for criticism only those major-generals who had independent commands and who botched the operations assigned to them. Major-General Townshend, who led the Tigris expedition in 1915–16, is the classic example.

The uncaring and stupid attitude of some very senior officers was typified by the general in command of Siegfried Sassoon's division, who forbade the wearing of steel helmets at the front because he considered that this might weaken the fighting spirit of his men. He also prohibited the issue of a rum ration before the commencement of an attack – though this order could be justified on the grounds that the liquor might make a man rash.

Captain John Glubb[4] of the Royal Engineers records how,

during the coldest months of the terrible winter of 1916–17, the men on his sector of the front were allowed no fuel for fires and forbidden to gather up the shell-shattered branches from a nearby wood. 'This was a most inhuman order', he writes, 'doubtless issued by some Q authority in a comfortable office at the base. The troops were perpetually wet through and could never get warm or dry. To be constantly cold is terribly depressing to morale.'

Arthur Behrand[5] reveals that it was not the habit of junior officers to criticise their top generals, 'for we did not know our generals, nor did they seem to want us to know them. I saw Haig but once and then only from a distance. Whatever the capacity of his brain, he looked the part and thus left one in no doubt that he was the sort of man well able to shoulder his responsibilities.'

All these generals whom I have listed were leaders of fighting formations but some other generals deserve history's censure. Some quartermaster-generals, adjutant-generals and chiefs-of-staff had little understanding of the conditions under which the men lived and fought. Some chaplain-generals, who might have been expected to show some feeling for the men were among the worst offenders. They had no military power or authority so they can hardly be blamed for bungling but some of their utterances about the war, especially after a major battle, were grotesque in their insensitivity.

The *Morning Post* graphically reported a statement by the Deputy Chaplain-General, Revd Llewellyn Gwynne, on the morning of 7 August 1916, by which time the Battle of the Somme had been careering bloodily out of control for more than five weeks:

To-morrow our troops scattered throughout France will attend solemn religious services, at which thanksgiving will be offered for all that Divine Providence has vouchsafed to us throughout the two years of this terrible war.
    A stirring message from the Deputy Chaplain-General lays down this final and greatest of lessons – that we are out to win, to fight for victory.

Once more then, English, Welsh, Scotch, Irish, Canadians, Australians, men of New Zealand, Newfoundland, Africa, India – once more look straight between the eyes of the bigness of our task, once more see the greatness of the stake, "once more into the breach, dear friends", and we shall keep for our children the Empire of our fathers. We shall free from tyranny Belgium and Serbia. We shall buy back with our blood justice and righteousness for Europe and lasting peace for the world.

Deputy Chaplain-General Gwynne had the example of the Archbishop of Canterbury to inspire him. 'Quit you like men', the Archbishop advised during a sermon on 2 May 1915. And he went on:

In the Greek it is one strong word. Hold and use what manhood stands for. The firm, well-set, thoughtful prowess into which the visions of boyhood have matured, the forcefulness which has outgrown the lad's light-hearted ardour while retaining its high spirit, the power that having stoutly vanquished thy enemies thou mayest not only receive the praise of this transient combat, but be crowned with the palm of eternal victory. Manhood at its best – unhesitating, persevering, undismayed.

This was ecclesiastical and spiritual arrogance. The soldiers needed some kind of understanding about what they were enduring on the battlefield, not patronising platitudes. The Archbishop may have been disturbed had he known that many men, though they persevered, did hesitate and were dismayed. He thought so much of his sermons that he published them and gave the booklet the title *Quit You Like Men*.

Just what Divine Providence had vouchsafed to the troops is difficult to discern and the Deputy Chaplain-General was not specific. He was certainly correct when he said that the soldiers saw 'the bigness' of the task. He was also right in the assumption that justice and righteousness would be bought back with British and Empire blood. It was repeatedly noticeable that the further from the front line a general was – whether a corps commander, an adjutant-general or a chaplain-general – the more lavishly he was prepared to shed other men's blood.

Not all British field generals were bunglers and there were some outstanding exceptions. General Sir Herbert Plumer, GOC 2nd Army, was a competent, careful commander and one ready to try new ideas. Plumer tried to minimise his casualties and though he did not always succeed it can be said that he did not throw away lives. Others who cannot be condemned as butchers or bunglers include General Sir Horace Smith-Dorrien and, with qualifications, General Sir Julian Byng. Field Marshal Lord Kitchener made some serious errors of judgment but was no butcher.

General Sir Frederick Maude, who recaptured Kut from the Turks and went on to take Baghdad from them, was no bungler. The Australian commander in France and Belgium, Lieut.-General Sir John Monash, was one of the most outstanding generals of the war. His compatriot, Lieut.-General Sir Harry Chauvel, led the Australian Light Horse in Palestine and could claim 36 victories in 36 engagements, with minimum loss of life to his own men. Lieut.-General Sir A.W. Currie, the Canadian commander, was a competent leader.

The British forces did not have a monopoly of butchers and bunglers. The French were handicapped by quite as many as the British, and the Germans, Russians and Italians had their share. However, this book is not about the generals of other nations and their incompetent leaders must be left to their historians.

Incompetent politicians appear in this book only because of their relationships with the generals. However, some of them deserve the censure of history for not being more decisive in controlling their generals.

No matter how hard historians strive to avoid making judgments by hindsight they cannot wholly succeed. In this book I have endeavoured to avoid the perils of hindsight by conceding the limitations, in 1914–18, of military development, of the professional training of officers and of the social system which so profoundly affected the thinking of generals about 'the men'. Where I am aware of criticism by hindsight, I say so.

Some of the generals whom I accuse of being bunglers and

butchers have their defenders. This applies particularly to Haig, whom some historians regard as one of history's 'Great Captains'. One calls him 'master of the battlefield'. That Haig should have defenders and apologists is interesting and worth explanation.

I have the impression that Haig saw God in his own image, and I am not the only one. Lytton Strachey, who witnessed the heartbreaking frontal assaults on the German trenches, was impatient with 'Haig's Scottish rigidity and the faith in a Haig-like god.' Perhaps Haig's defenders see more virtue in his rigidity and faith than do Strachey and I.

I believe, that 70 years after the war ended, the memory of the old Empire's one million servicemen who did not return home and the suffering of millions more who did, demands the truth about the senior leadership. The time for cover-ups, for pleas in mitigation, for apologetics and rationalisation, and for parading extenuating circumstances and good intentions is long past. Whether Haig and Hunter-Weston, Hamilton and Haking, French and Harper were considerate husbands and kind fathers is not relevant to a study of them as military commanders. Their personal–private qualities cannot be used as factors for mitigation to offset their feelings on the battlefield.

I do not criticise the generals' personal courage. With a single major exception, they were brave men and had proved themselves to be so when of junior rank. As senior generals they were rarely exposed to enemy fire – nor should they have been. A general in a front-line trench during a battle would have been guilty of dereliction of duty. Even so, had generals visited the front trenches during quiet periods they would have been showing a real sense of leadership.

There are photographs which show generals in trenches but they were generally rear trenches or enemy positions which had been overrun. King George V and the Prince of Wales are to be seen in trenches, with generals as an escort but, naturally, the positions were considered very safe.

That the Allies were at long last victorious had little to do with qualities of generalship. Most of the field-marshals and generals who took part in the great victory parades did not deserve the honours and rewards heaped upon them. Having organised and presided over the destruction of a generation, they were simply in the right place when the German will for war finally broke.

That it did break was the result of several factors. One was the effect of the British naval blockade of German ports, so that the population suffered from acute shortages of basic food and supplies. Another was the entry of the United States into the war and the imminent use of hundreds of thousands, perhaps millions, of fresh men. The German leaders could see that this weight of manpower would be overwhelming. In addition, political manoeuvring within Germany led to what the army called 'the stab in the back'. The German army suffered reverses and by October 1918 it was being steadily pushed back, but it was not a beaten army and it was never required to fight a battle on German soil. Neither Haig nor the Allied Supreme Commander, Marshal Foch, were 'masters of the battlefield' by their own endeavours.

The British government, people and army were so relieved that victory had finally come to the battered Allies that they would have applauded any man who happened to be the commander-in-chief at the time. Haig's greatest achievement was to remain as commander-in-chief despite his reverses and enormous losses. In the following great war any reverse on the same scale and any great loss of men would have resulted in dismissal of a senior commander. Haig triumphed over his own political leaders – really his superiors – and this was a considerable feat. He proved that, as Keith Robbins[6] discerns, 'Diplomats were only the handmaidens of warriors. It was the course of the fighting which shaped the choices they had to make.'

As the war ended there came the poetic idea of the 'Unknown Warrior', the victim who would forever represent all the dead servicemen of the war. A blindfolded British officer 'of very high rank' – a general, in fact – was led into a hut containing the remains of six unidentified soldiers brought from the various battlefronts. He then groped about alone until he touched a coffin. This was the one taken back to Westminster Abbey and buried with all the honours that the nation could provide.

The event was a symbolism of sacrifice at its best, a magnificent idea. It was also entirely fitting. Blinkered generals, blind to the realities of war, had caused the shocking casualties. It was appropriate that one of them should choose the man to represent all the soldiers who had been butchered.

NOTES

1. A.J.P. Taylor, *In the First World War*, Hamish Hamilton, London, 1963. Born in 1906, he was a Fellow of Magdalen College and lectured there on modern history.
2. Arthur Russell, *The Machine Gunner*, Roundwood Press, 1977. Russell enlisted in 1915 at the age of 18 and served with 98 Machine Gun Company on the Somme and in the Ypres Salient.
3. Norman F. Dixon, *On the Psychology of Military Incompetence*. Jonathan Cape, London, 1976. After 10 years in the Royal Engineers, Dixon left the army in 1950. He was awarded the MBE. A Doctor of Science and of Philosophy, he became Reader in Psychology at University College, London.
4. John Glubb, *Into Battle*, London, 1928. Glubb became a major-general and commanded Jordan's Arab Legion.
5. Arthur Behrand, *As From Kemmel Hill*, Eyre & Spottiswoode, 1963. Adjutant of an Artillery Brigade, Behrand also wrote *Make Me a Soldier*.
6. Keith Robbins, *The First World War*, Oxford University Press, 1984. Robbins is Professor of Modern History at the University of Glasgow.

2

The BUTCHER'S BILL

Samples

The 1st Battalion the Queen's Royal Regiment (West Surrey), of 850 men, fought in the Battle of Gheluvelt, Ypres, 31 October 1914. These were the survivors:

Battalion HQ:	Nil	
A Company:	2	corporals, 2 lance-corporals,
	20	privates
B Company:	4	privates
C Company:	2	privates
D Company:	1	lance-corporal, 1 private

The group was commanded by Lieut. John Boyd, the only surviving officer.

At the end of First Ypres, 18 November 1914, the British Expeditionary Force had virtually ceased to exist. Of the first 100,000 soldiers who had gone to France in August, one-third lay under the soil of France and Belgium. The average strength of the original battalions was 1 officer and 30 men, instead of 40 officers and 1,000 men.

At Neuve Chapelle, Flanders, the British army lost 13,000 men between 10–13 March 1915. The 2nd Battalion Middlesex Regiment was virtually wiped out by two German machine-gun posts.

BUTCHERS AND BUNGLERS

During the Second Ypres, 22 April–25 May, 1915, British casualties amounted to 50,000. The 10th Brigade lost 73 officers and 2,346 men and practically ceased to exist. The 149th Brigade lost 42 officers and 1,192 men, three-quarters of its complement.

The Gallipoli campaign began on 25 April 1915 and ended in January 1916. Total British casualties were about 205,000, including 43,000 killed or dead of wounds or disease; 90,000 were evacuated sick. Within these overall figures are 26,094 Australian casualties, including 7,594 killed, and 7,571 New Zealand casualties, including 2,431 killed. The campaign achieved nothing.

During Second Krithia, Gallipoli, 8 May 1915 the 2nd Australian Brigade went into an assault with 2,900 men and lost 1,056, including 16 officers killed and 32 wounded. In the 6th Battalion only one of the original combatant officers was left.

Between 22 November 1914 and 29 April 1916 35,000 British and Indian troops were lost in abortive campaigns in Mesopotamia (now Iraq).

On 9 May 1915, at Aubers Ridge in French Flanders, just 15 German companies and 22 machine-guns stopped in their tracks three attacking British brigades – about 10,000 men. Only 50 men of the 1st Battalion Black Watch reached the enemy parapets. Total British casualties were 27,000. The strategic gain was nil, the tactical gain negligible.

On the first day of the Battle of Loos, northern France, 25 September 1915, the 15th Division lost 60 per cent of its men and several of its battalions were destroyed. The 6th Cameron Highlanders went in with 28 officers and 1,000 men. One officer, a junior subaltern, survived to bring out 40 men. On the second day 12 fresh battalions, about 10,000 men in all, launched a new attack. In 210 minutes' fighting they lost 385 officers and 7,861 men. Total British casualties by the end of the battle, 8 October, were 60,000.

THE BUTCHER'S BILL

On the first day of the Battle of the Somme, 1 July 1916, 20,000 British soldiers were killed and another 40,000 wounded. The names of the dead take up 212 pages in a record book. From Bradford alone there were 1,770 casualties in the first hour of the offensive. The 1st Newfoundland Battalion, 850 men, was thrown into an attack near Beaumont Hamel. It suffered 700 casualties, the men being 'mown down in heaps'.

In one night's fighting at Fromelles in French Flanders, 20–21 July 1916, the Australian 5th Division suffered 5,533 casualties, more than a quarter of its strength. Nothing was achieved by the attack.

In six weeks on Poziéres Ridge, July–August 1916, the Australian 1st, 2nd and 4th Divisions lost 23,000 men killed or wounded. General Haig said, 'Luckily, their [the Australians] losses have been fairly small'.

On 15 July the South African Brigade went into action at Delville Wood, Somme, with 121 officers and 3,032 men. On 20 July just 29 officers and 751 men came out. The Germans still held most of the wood.

'The blind boy with both legs off is dying; he doesn't know his legs are off, and is cheerfully delirious most of the time. He calls us "Teacher," and says, "Look sharp, dear, go and get it now." He was murmuring "Such is life" just now.' Nursing Sister K.E. Luard, in a letter of 16 September 1916.

When the Battle of the Somme ended on 18 November 1916 the British and Empire armies had suffered 420,000 casualties. On the entire British–French front only 125 square miles of country had been taken from the Germans.

In capturing Vimy Ridge, 9 April 1917, the Canadians suffered 11,000 casualties.

On the night of 10–11 April 1917 units of the Australian 4th Division were committed to an attack at Bullecourt, northern France. They suffered more than 3,000 casualties, 2,339 in the 4th Brigade alone.

Second Bullecourt raged between 3–26 May 1917. Thirty-two Australian battalions of roughly 24,000 men were engaged and they suffered 7,000 casualties. The Australians captured and held a position within the enemy's Hindenburg Line, but with neither strategic nor tactical advantage.

By mid-1917 wounded soldiers had become a familiar sight all over Britain. Visiting Brighton, Sussex, in June, Caroline Playne wrote, 'The sight of hundreds of men on crutches going about in groups, many having lost one leg, many others both legs, caused sickening horror. The maiming of masses of strong young men thus brought home was appalling.' According to Mrs Playne – in her book *Britain Holds On* – people became so used to such sights that there was a 'hardening and coarsening of national life'. Of course, the public were seeing survivors; they would have been much more sickened by the corpses on the battlefields.

The 36th (Ulster) Division lost 144 officers and 3,441 men in the period 2–18 August 1917.

Between 21 March and 4 April 1918 a German offensive cost the Allies 160,000 casualties and 70,000 men as prisoners.

Third Ypres began on 31 July 1917. When it ended on 6 November the British and Empire Armies had suffered at least 400,000 casualties. No strategic gain had been achieved.

The British–French allies waged a pointless and intermittently active campaign in Salonika between 1915 and 1918. The British reported 481,000 cases of illness and 23,000 other casualties.

During the fighting on the Western Front, 1914–18, the British and Empire armies lost 118,941 officers and 2,571,113 men as battle casualties. Others became casualties through illness. More than half of all British and Empire soldiers on the Western Front suffered some kind of wound in battle.

Oxford University's Roll of Honour contains 14,561 names; of these 2,680 were killed or died of wounds or sickness. Trinity College, Cambridge lost more than 600 of its former graduates. The London & North Western Railway Company had 3,840 of its staff killed in action. Nearly 500 former pupils of Tonbridge School, Kent were killed.

Between the outbreak of war and the end of 1918 a total of 304 British soldiers were executed by firing squad. Of these, 19 had been found guilty of murder and for that offence death was the penalty in civil life as in the services. The other offences which applied only to the armed forces and for which death was the ultimate penalty were desertion, cowardice, quitting a post when on duty, disobedience, striking a superior officer, casting away arms, mutiny and sleeping on post. By far the greatest number of executions were carried out for the crime of desertion, while 16 men were shot for what was considered cowardice. Many hundreds of British soldiers deserted through fear and were not caught, so escaping punishment. Not all those who did desert were executed. Perhaps the most significant figure which does not appear in war statistics concerns the tens of thousands of men who only just managed *not* to run away. They may have been the most genuine heroes of the war.

3

DEDICATED
FUTILITY

'Bloody Balls-up'

ROBERT GRAVES, GOODBYE TO ALL THAT

Field-Marshal Sir John French was irascible, moody, vindictive, weak and inefficient, not altogether the man to lead the British Expeditionary Force to war, but then he was the ranking general.* His own two senior officers were Lieut.-General Sir Horace Smith-Dorrien, commanding 11 Corps and Lieut.-General Sir Douglas Haig, commanding 1 Corps.

Haig wanted French's job and as early as 11 August 1914, only a week after the outbreak of war, he began to undermine his chief. French and Haig, both cavalrymen, shared only one thing – detestation of the other. Haig was scornful of French's military knowledge, despised his character and personality and shied away from his volatile temper. 'In my heart', he wrote in his diary, 'I know that French is quite unfit for this great command at a time of crisis in our nation's history.' Just who might be better fitted he did not say, but his friends knew of his great ambitions.

---

*   Before French became Commander-in-Chief, it is said that he borrowed from the War Office library Hamley's *Operations of War*, but could not understand it. He never asked for another book, but this may have been merely coincidental. One of his contemporaries believed that he had read 'a few' military books but did not follow them.

While motoring around the lines at Aldershot with King George V, he told the king that he had grave doubts whether French's temper was 'sufficiently even or his military knowledge sufficiently thorough to enable him to discharge properly the very difficult duties which will devolve upon him during the coming operations.' According to Haig's diary entry of that day, he 'thought it sufficient to tell the king that he had doubts' about French's selection. It would have been unlike George V not to press Haig for details about these doubts, but French had so far done nothing to justify dismissal.

Having set up his GHQ – 35 miles from where the fighting was taking place – Sir John French called formally upon his battlefront neighbour, General Lanrezac, Commander of the French Fifth Army. Their meeting may have been the most disastrous military–social encounter of the war. Through insensitivity, stupidity or inflexibility – perhaps all three – the two generals took an instant dislike to each other. Sir John spoke no French and regarded the entire French nation as unreliable, dishonest and chauvinistic. Lanrezac spoke no English and considered all Englishmen stubborn, arrogant and unreliable. Sir John refused to make any concessions to his French confrére and after the first meeting wanted nothing to do with him socially or militarily. In this way the British and the French went to war together against a common enemy, who was forcing both of them to retreat.

At one critical point in the retreat Lanrezac sent a captain to Haig's HQ saying that he intended to give battle the next morning and asking for British support. At the same time a British airman had landed near British HQ to report that German columns had been observed advancing rapidly south-west of St Quentin. Haig marked the French captain's map and said: 'Return quickly to your general with this information. He should take advantage of it at once. The Germans are exposing their flank as they advance. I am anxious to co-operate in this attack.'

Haig realised that his tired infantry needed a few hours rest and sent a message to Sir John French to that effect. He added that he could offer the French the support of his artillery and machine-

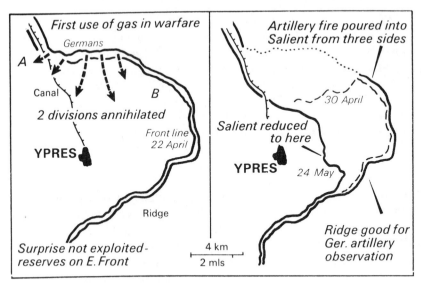

Second battle of Ypres, 1915

guns if the Commander-in-Chief approved. French replied: 'No active operations of any arms except of a defensive nature will be undertaken tomorrow.'

This was the first opportunity for Allied co-operation in the field – and it was thrown away. Next day the French fought the Battle of Guise, without help from the BEF.

The following day the petulant Sir John French sent a curt message to Haig: 'Please be good enough to inform the C-in-C how it is that any confidential promise of support by 1 Corps was made to General Lanrezac or why official exchange of ideas was initiated without authority from Headquarters.'

Haig's response was a stinging snub: 'I do not understand what you mean. I have initiated no exchange of ideas. GHQ not having secured from the French any roads for the retirement of my Corps, I had for my own safety to enter into relations with the nearest French force on my right. As far as it was possible I have maintained touch with the left of these French troops – and due to the presence of the Corps their left has been protected since we left Maubeuge. My Corps still protects their left, and if the enemy advances from St Quentin southward I shall have for my own safety to deploy guns etc. without asking for the authority of GHQ. The extrication of this Corps from the false position in which it is placed still demands the greatest exertion from us all, and my sole objective is to secure its retreat with honour to our arms. I therefore beg you will not give credit to such allegations as the one under reference without first ascertaining whether it is true or not.'

Next day Haig, still angry, drove to his C-in-C personally and squeezed an apology out of him. Having alienated the French commanders, Sir John had now upset one of his two Corps commanders, both of them soon to be Army Commanders.

According to the Official Historian of the Western Front campaigns, Brigadier-General H.E. Edmonds, Haig was French's favourite, hence he wanted to block those officers who might be rivals to Haig. This, says Edmonds, explains his hostile attitude towards Smith-Dorrien.

At the battle of Mons on 23 August Sir John gave the order, 'The BEF will give battle on the line of the Conde [Mons] canal.'

Smith-Dorrien asked, 'Do you mean to take the offensive or stand on the defensive?' This was a valid, sensible and justifiable question.

French walked away and whispered with his Chief-of-Staff, Sir Archibald Murray, and then returned to Smith-Dorrien. 'You do as you are ordered', he exclaimed, 'and don't ask questions!' The incident illustrates the pettiness and stupidity of the BEF's commander.

Smith-Dorrien made contact with the advancing German army at Le Cateau and French ordered him to retreat. Realising that to do so would jeopardise the safety of the entire BEF, Smith-Dorrien ignored GHQ and engaged the enemy. Had Smith-Dorrien retired, Haig's Corps would have been left with its left flank exposed to the full fury of the German attack. Out of touch with his distant Commander-in-Chief, Smith-Dorrien had no alternative but to fight. It was a tremendous task, because both his flanks were 'in the air' and the Germans outnumbered him by two to one. Yet Smith-Dorrien checked the Germans. After the war the great German general whom he had blocked, von Kluck, said, 'The way the retreat was carried out was remarkable. I tried very hard to outflank the BEF but could not do so. If I had succeeded the war would have been won.'

Instead of being enveloped, the army, weary but intact, withdrew to fight another day. In short, Smith-Dorrien had rescued French from his own incompetence, the results of which could have been catastrophic.

The King congratulated Smith-Dorrien but the Commander-in-Chief did not at once send his thanks and congratulations. Mean and insecure, French was jealous of the soldierly and competent Smith-Dorrien and disliked him intensely. Sir John had little idea of what was going on at the front and when he withdrew his GHQ a further 35 miles to the rear, he had no idea whatsoever. However, he formed the opinion that Smith-Dorrien's troops were running from the Germans, who were in hot pursuit. This called for incisive action so French sent a signal that all spare ammunition and officers' kits should be abandoned. This fatuous order astounded Corps HQ. Smith-Dorrien and his staff knew that if the officers abandoned their baggage the troops might well believe that a retreat was about to begin and as a result their morale would fall. Smith-Dorrien simply ignored the order, on the charitable assumption that French could not be expected to know that at the front everything was under control.

For the second time, Smith-Dorrien had saved Sir John French from his own blunders. The touchy Commander-in-Chief now disliked the 'insubordinate' 11 Corps commander even more intensely – but how to get rid of such a respected leader? He could not even prevent his promotion to command the Second Army.

French was constantly looking over his shoulder and distrusted the Secretary of State for War, Lord Kitchener, as much as he did Smith-Dorrien. He felt that his features rather than those of Kitchener should have been on the famous recruiting poster which challenged Britain's men. He also feared that Kitchener, who spoke fluent French, might make arrangements with the French leaders behind his back.

On 14 October the German commander, General Erich von Falkenbayn, sent his Fourth and Sixth Armies against British-held Ypres. They pressed forward for 9 days and were finally halted by French reinforcements rushed to the area and by the Belgians, on the left, who flooded their front by opening the sluice gates from Dixmuide to the sea. Heavy rain and snow brought the battle to an end on 11 November, with the British holding a salient 6 miles deep into the German lines – but the Germans held all the high ground.

At one point in the battle French went to see General Foch and told him, 'I have no more reserves. The only men I have left are the sentries at my gates. I will take them with me to where the line is broken, and the last of the English will die fighting.'[1]

He was not far from the literal truth. The battle cost him 2,368 officers and 55,787 men – 80 per cent of the men in his original BEF.

Early in 1915 the French commander, Marshal Joseph Joffre, requested that British units relieve the two French corps which had taken over the Ypres Salient. Sir John decided on a strong attack before agreeing to this and on 10 March he opened one of the war's first great artillery barrages. The targets were the German positions in and around the village of Neuve Chapelle. The bombardment was followed with an assault by troops of Haig's First Army. British and Indian infantry captured the ruins but neither Haig, more or less on the spot, nor French, further back, pressed the unexpected advantage. General von Falken-bayn rushed 16,000 reinforcements to the spot and on 13 March French halted the British offensive. Having captured 400 acres at a cost of 13,000 casualties he claimed a great victory.

In truth, Neuve Chapelle was nearly a success and might have been counted a valuable experiment had the British and French High Commands learnt from it. They deduced that a great volume of shellfire was the key to success. The real lesson was that a short and very intense bombardment could achieve tactical surprise. The generals also did not see – or did not act upon – the associated lesson that the enemy sector attacked should be sufficiently wide to prevent the Germans' artillery from commanding the breach and their infantry reserves from closing it. It was the end of 1917 before the British reverted to the Neuve Chapelle method.

On 22 April 1915 the Germans attacked at Ypres with chlorine gas – a new and fearsome weapon. It should not have taken the Allies by surprise for Intelligence had information from many sources that such an attack was imminent. No steps were taken to meet the threat and no warnings were given. Casualties were few but frightening. As French Moroccan troops fell back in disorder Smith-Dorrien's Second Army found itself outflanked right and left on the frontline of the Ypres Salient.

Smith-Dorrien wrote a careful, logical appreciation of the situation. Counter-attacks would be costly and futile, he pointed out, and he suggested a withdrawal to a new defence line west of Ypres. In making this professional appraisal he unavoidably gave Sir John French the chance to trap him. Charging Smith-Dorrien with not only having disobeyed his orders but with being a source of 'dangerous pessimism', he forced his resignation. The man who was probably the British Army's most able and professionally-minded general left the field.

A few days after Smith-Dorrien's departure – his sacking disguised as a return home because of ill-health – French authorised General Sir Herbert Plumer to withdraw as Smith-Dorrien had proposed. The historian A.J. Smithers says, 'There is no accounting for how a man in so high a position could behave thus, or how a man capable of such behaviour could have been placed in so high a position.'

At this time French's command had been more marked by bungling than butchery – though there had been plenty of that too. The BEF suffered 60,000 casualties in its defence of Ypres, largely because French personally ordered units into hopeless attacks across open ground. It has to be said that the Germans, with the initiative still in their hands and a greater weight of men and weapons, could only be checked by dogged British and French resistance.

In the Ypres fighting the Allies had lost a 2-mile zone to the north and east but French nevertheless decided that the terribly vulnerable and much reduced British salient was worth holding.

This decision, made without an attempt to foresee the probable progress of the war, was to have bloody consequences.

Attention now switched to the French front at Vimy Ridge, 50 miles south of Ypres. In gallant but foolish frontal assaults, the French suffered 100,000 casualties and though they inflicted 75,000 casualties on the Germans they could make no progress against the enemy's machine-guns and cleverly sited trenches. What the French could attempt, so could the British, and on 9 May Haig's First Army attacked Aubers Ridge, actually rising ground only a few hundred feet above sea level.

That month, with the war in progress 10 months and the Germans' defensive techniques well understood by the British and French, Haig let it be known that the way to capture machine-guns was by grit, determination and the qualities of the stalker.[2] Grit and determination were certainly necessary but Haig's references to the 'qualities of the stalker' gives the impression that he saw a German machine-gun post as roughly the equivalent in terms of danger as a wild animal. Capturing a machine-gun required firepower, tactical skill, a supply of grenades, a knowledge of how a German machine-gun crew operated and a lot of luck – as well as grit and determination.

The German defenders could not credit what they were seeing – British soldiers climbing from their trenches into the open and advancing steadily to almost certain death against machine-guns. The attack was called off the same day, but in response to requests from the French some other equally abortive British attacks were made on Aubers Ridge – without any change in tactics.

During the Aubers Ridge battle one of Haig's Corps Commanders, General Sir Henry Rawlinson, was angered by the apparent absence of the East Lancashires and the Sherwood Foresters. The situation was 'most unsatisfactory', he declared and furiously he demanded to know where they were. A brigade commander said, 'They are lying out in No-Man's-Land, sir, and most of them will never stand again.'

Meanwhile, other British and French troops had been landed at Gallipoli, where the leaders made no more progress than those on the Western Front. Allied statesmen agreed that while fresh efforts were made at Gallipoli during the summer, warfare in France and Belgium would be allowed to simmer. If no progress was made at Gallipoli then a fresh offensive would take place in northern France. For reasons explained elsewhere no progress *was* made at Gallipoli.

The British were to attack at Loos, an area of coal mines and slag heaps, just the place for a battle. In fact, Sir John French and Haig did not like the place but Kitchener overruled them. Losses would be heavy, Kitchener recognised this, but everything must be done, he said, to support the French army which was to attack at the same time in Champagne.

While he might have had misgivings about the chosen battlefield, Haig was confident. 'We shall win', he told Lieut.-General Hubert Gough, quoting from scripture, ' "not by power or might, but by *My Spirit*, saith the Lord of Hosts".' He hoped that poison gas, a new weapon in British hands, would assist the Lord of Hosts in securing victory.

For the battle on 25 September Sir John French stationed himself at Lillers, 25 miles from his own Chief-of-Staff, General Sir William Robertson. French did not even have a telephone, a dereliction of duty at high level and a blunder that could not be excused. French went further down the blunderer's path. He insisted on keeping the reserve corps under his own hand. His reason for this was that two of the reserve's divisions, the 21st and 24th, were among the first of Kitchener's New Armies to reach France and were totally inexperienced. French did not want to throw them straight into battle. He was also motivated by jealousy of Haig.

Haig knew that he was taking a risk with gas, the new weapon. The army's special gas companies, about 1,400 men, filed into the British line on the evening of 24 April to man more than 400 gas emplacements. They would discharge chlorine gas and smoke intermittently for 40 minutes before the assault – should the wind be favourable. If it were unfavourable then the guns, with insufficient ammunition, would have to do the job unaided.

The final decision had to be made at 3 a.m. Haig ordered the discharge to take place at 5 a.m. but the breeze was then slight and Haig contacted his Corps commanders about delaying the attack. It was now too late for this.

It was the first British operation of its kind and problems abounded. In some places, bursting enemy shells buried gas personnel and their cylinders; elsewhere pipes and cylinders were broken. Many cylinders proved to be defective. To counter the gas leakages in the British trenches, Vermorel sprayers had been provided for decontamination but they proved to be useless.

With the wind now dangerous, some gas officers stopped the discharge on their own initiative. On the left of the line gas officers were ordered by divisional headquarters to continue discharging and the gas drifted across the trenches and hung there. Conditions were terrible for British and Germans. Men of the British 2nd Division returned choking to their own trenches.

The German machine-gunners wore oxygen apparatus, infinitely more efficient equipment than that possessed by the British or even by the German riflemen. Their guns swept the bare terrain, catching swarms of British soldiers, many of them confused and disoriented by the gas and smoke. Lieut. Robert Graves of the Royal Welsh Fusiliers, going into the battle, found the whole situation confused. Meeting some walking-wounded of the Middlesex Regiment stumbling back to a dressing-station, he demanded 'What's happened? What's happened?'[3]

The most detailed answer he could get was 'Bloody balls-up'.

About 130,000 men had started the attack; at nightfall 15,470 were dead or wounded. Some of Haig's troops had taken a part of the German front line, a few were even further into enemy territory, but reserves were desperately needed for the next day's fighting. French understood the overall position at 11 a.m. on 25 September, but not having a telephone in his GHQ, went to talk with Haig. He told Haig that he had decided to lend him the 21st and 24th Divisions from XI Corps to support the attack.

Road control was poor and the 21st and 24th Divisions, eager but apprehensive, had to make four exhausting night marches to reach the front. They needed rest and were not ready until midday on 26 April. As always, the Germans moved more rapidly. The High Command rushed 22 more battalions into the trenches. Without having eaten for 60 hours, because no food was available, the 21st and 24th were thrown into the fighting. In full light, the gallant and spirited, but untrained troops advanced in close order across open ground swept by machine-gun fire and deluged by shellfire.

The Germans of the XV Reserve Regiment who opposed the 24th Division could hardly believe that they had such a target. When their regimental diarist came to describe the event he was still verbally breathless:

> Ten ranks of extended line could clearly be distinguished, each one estimated at more than a thousand men, and offering such a target as had never been seen before, or even thought possible. Never had the machine-gunners such straightforward work to do nor done it so effectively. They traversed to and fro along the enemy's ranks unceasingly. The men stood on the firestep, some even on the parapets, and fired exultantly into the mass of men advancing across the open grassland. As the entire field of fire was covered with the enemy's infantry the effect was devastating and they could be seen falling in hundreds.

A German Regimental Diary refers to the 21st Division's sector:

> Dense masses of infantry, line after line, came into sight on the ridge, some of their officers even mounted on horseback, and advancing as if carrying out a field-day drill in peacetime. Our artillery and machine-guns riddled their ranks as they came on. As they crossed the northern front of Hugo Wood the machine-guns positioned there caught them in the flank and whole battalions must have been utterly destroyed. The English made five consecutive attempts to press on past the wood and reach our second defence position, but finally, weakened by their terrible losses, they were forced to give in.

The 24th, led by inspired junior leadership and heroic effort, reached the German second line. Only a few hand wire cutters had been issued and the men with them could not cut the tough steel barbed wire. Some desperate men threw themselves onto the wire in a vain attempt to crush it; others attempted to climb over it, others tugged at it. All died on it.

The commander of a German battalion is reported to have said: 'The massacre filled every one of us watching with a sense of disgust and nausea.' The Germans did not fire at the British soldiers who tried to crawl or limp back to their lines. During the day a German officer called the place 'The Corpse Field of Loos' and the name has remained in German military history. The Germans took in many wounded but others were left lying on the ground in front of the wire, calling out, lifting their arms and crying for help.

The two British divisions had gone into battle with a strength of 10,000 men. In 200 minutes they lost 385 officers and 7,861 men. The Germans had so few casualties they were not reported.

The Lord of Hosts, on whom Haig had depended, had been conspicuously absent from his side during the fighting, but Haig may have been able to rationalise that the ill-will of his Commander-in-Chief was a greater force than the goodwill of the Lord of Hosts. In any case, he and French ploughed on amid the slag heaps. On 27 September grenade throwers were sent forward, ahead of the usual charge, to clear enemy dugouts in an attempt to seize The Dump, a dominating slag heap. An officer of the 12th Royal Fusiliers saw part of the ferocious action:

> Over the edge they found the machine-gun bullets playing breast high and felt the sing of bullets about their ears. Men flung up their arms and toppled backwards. 'Where are those bombers? Bloody hell! Where are those bombers?' It was the sergeant-major. There was a catch in his voice as he realised that the bombers had been caught by the machine-guns; that the attack was doomed to failure.

Still the British command, with French compliance elsewhere in Artois, went on pushing. On 13 October, four British divisions made the last serious attack at Loos. A single division suffered 3,800 casualties, mostly in the first 10 minutes. In all, the British had lost 61,280 soldiers.

Even after the machine-gun was obviously dominating the battlefield – obvious because of the casualties it was causing among British troops – French and Haig resisted the suggestion that the pre-war scale of two to a battalion should be increased. Haig stated that the machine-gun was 'a much over-rated weapon' and that two to a battalion was ample. Even Kitchener, who had more foresight than most generals, laid down that four were a maximum and any more than this a luxury. It was Lloyd George as Minister of Munitions who saved the soldiers by raising the scale to 16 to a battalion, without referring the matter to the Army chiefs.

The British High Command claimed Loos as a victory. The British leaders also claimed that they had bought experience. The survivors had; the experience was not much use to the dead. Nobody seemed to realise that the Germans had also gained experience, at a much cheaper price. And they showed much more promise of using it than did the British.

In fact, the Loos offensive was a total failure, partly caused by French's inept handling of the reserve. His despatch, describing the battle, seemed to imply that Haig was to blame. Haig decided that now was the time for a change and he relayed his unflattering views on French to Lord Esher, Prime Minister Asquith and other Cabinet members. French's own Chief-of-Staff, Robertson, turned against him and intrigued with Haig to have him removed.

Haig had ready access to the King, partly because his wife was a lady-in-waiting to the Queen. The King invited Haig to his room to discuss Sir John French's leadership. Haig's diary entry for 24 October 1915 describes the occasion and his own 'complete candour':

> I told him that I thought the time to have removed French was after the Retreat, because he had so mismanaged matters and shown . . .
> a great ignorance of the essential principles of war. Since then, during the trench warfare, the Army had grown larger and I thought at first there was no great scope for French to go wrong. But French's handling of the reserves in the last battle [Loos] his obstinacy, and conceit, showed his incapacity and it seemed to me impossible for anyone to prevent him doing the same thing again. I

therefore thought strongly, that for the sake of the Empire, French ought to be removed. I personally, was ready to do my duty in any capacity . . . .

Haig believed that the King's attitude, as a result of this talk, did much to bring about a change in the High Command. Early in December Prime Minister Asquith dismissed French. There could be no doubt as to his successor – Haig himself. He took over command on 19 December 1915.

Simultaneously with Haig's advancement, his good friend Sir William Robertson became Chief of the Imperial General Staff, with so much power that the post of CIGS was no longer subordinate to the Secretary of State for War, Lord Kitchener. As CIGS, Robertson was principal military adviser to the Government with direct access to the War Cabinet. Kitchener declined into a mere figurehead with no real control over events. Haig could depend on Robertson's unqualified support for his opinion that the major war effort must be waged on the Western Front and with no 'diversions' elsewhere.

French's defenders say that Haig was satisfied with the arrangements made for the placement of the reserves at Loos, also that they moved off within 45 minutes of Haig's request for them being received at GHQ. Whatever the truth of those particular points, French falsified dates and times in his despatches.

The bitter Sir John, who had greatly assisted Haig's career, was mollified with a home command and an earldom. He became Earl of Ypres. As he had cooperated with the Germans in destroying the British army at and around that place it was appropriate. Haig's assessment of Sir John French as a military commander can hardly be disputed. Impetuous, petty, and unbalanced, he had been left in command of a fine army for far too long – 17 months. The Prime Minister should have dismissed him long before.

Having criticised French for making the same mistakes over and over again, Haig continued with precisely the same tactics as French – and on a much larger scale.

BUTCHERS AND BUNGLERS

NOTES

1. Brigadier-General E.L. Spears, a senior liaison officer on French's staff, wrote about the incident in *Liaison 1914*.
2. Haig Diary, 20 May 1915. WO 256/4 PRO.
3. Robert Graves, one of the war's finest poets, wrote vividly about his experience in *Goodbye to All That*.

Comments and statements by Haig may be read in his diary, in letters to his wife, in his despatches and in Brigadier-General John Charteris' book *At G.H.Q.*

4

GALLIPOLI FIASCO

'Singularly Brainless Warfare'

JOHN NORTH, GALLIPOLI: THE FADING VISION

Few places have so many natural advantages for defence as Turkey's Gallipoli peninsula and the Dardanelles, the narrow strait which separates the peninsula from Turkey's Asiatic mainland. However, for reasonable strategic reasons, the British and French decided to attack these targets. Since Turkey was an ally of the Germans and Austrians, the Allied objective was to create another front at the rear of the Central Powers, thus forcing them to divert forces from the Western and the Russian fronts. Should Constantinople (Istanbul) be captured Turkey would be forced out of the war.

No military or naval intelligence appreciation of the Gallipoli–Dardanelles situation was ever made, not even at strategic level. Had such an analysis been attempted it might have shown that no serious naval or military attack was necessary. Major-General Sir Charles Calwell, an astute Director of Military Operations, believed that 'so long as they are more or less threatened, the Dardanelles and Constantinople placed a trump card in the hands of the Allies.' His point was that without risking a ship or a soldier the Entente Powers could have kept the great Turkish forces occupied. The weapon would have been bluff. Winston Churchill, as First Lord of the Admiralty, preferred invasion of

Gallipoli and penetration of the Dardanelles, and he had his supporters.

After abortive British and French naval attacks and bombardments all hopes of a surprise military landing vanished. The British had considered neither tactics nor logistics and until 12 March 1915 no commander had been selected for the contemplated field force. Kitchener chose General Sir Ian Hamilton. Cultured, wealthy and gifted, Hamilton was sixty-two and had more active service on his record than any other senior serving British officer. However, he had not been to France – the enmity of Sir John French and others had seen to that.* Not that Hamilton was a dangerous competitor to them for high command. He was too personally charming, too balanced and too lacking in ruthlessness. These same qualities made him unsuitable for a high and independent command abroad. Hamilton himself was startled by the appointment, but this was his last chance to win great military fame and retire as a field-marshal.

He set off for the Mediterranean equipped with two small tourist guidebooks on Western Turkey, an out-of-date and inaccurate map never intended for military use and a 1905 textbook on the Turkish army. Kitchener had denied him any aircraft, which were vital for reconnaissance in an unknown area. He had only two assets, one of which was the able General Sir William Birdwood, who had expected to be given command of the force. The other was the experienced British 29th Division. Neither Hamilton nor anyone else could yet know that the Australian and New Zealand soldiers destined to fight at Gallipoli would prove to be some of the finest soldiers on either side during the war. Birdwood was their GOC.

From the little liaison which took place between the French and British over the Gallipoli campaign they might not have been

---

* Hamilton had crossed Haig towards the end of the Boer War when he pointed out, in an official memorandum, that the old cavalry tactics were dead and that the true function of the horse was to convey a rifleman to a point of attack or move him rapidly through a zone of fire. Haig and French resented being taught their business by an infantryman and training methods were not changed.

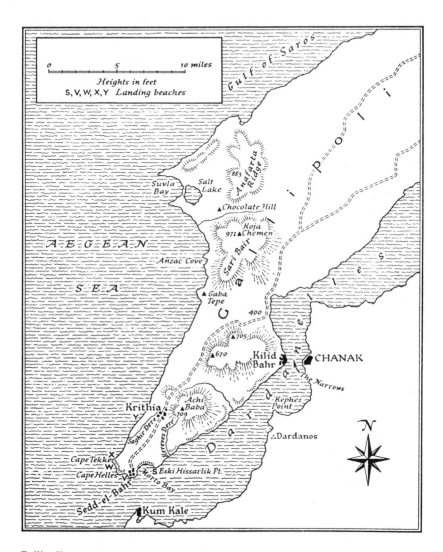

Gallipoli

fighting as allies. To lead the French contingent, Marshal Joffre choose General Albert d'Amade, who had already shown on the Western Front that he was not fitted for a difficult role. In fact, he had been removed from his post for gross dereliction of duty.

Hamilton saw the peninsula for the first time from the deck of a ship and wrote to Kitchener: 'Gallipoli looks a much tougher nut to crack than it did over a map in your office.' In an attempt to crack it he decided on a double blow against the southern half of the peninsula, plus three feint attacks. Not long before the invasion he added two more landings. They were at Y Beach on the Aegean coast and S Beach at the northern end of Morto Bay. Overall commander in the south, at Cape Helles, was GOC 29th Division, Major-General Sir Aylmer Hunter-Weston.

On 21 April Hamilton issued a 'general address' and instructed that it be read to all troops:

> Before us lies an adventure unprecedented in modern warfare. Together with our comrades of the fleet we are about to force a landing upon an open beach in face of positions which have been vaunted by our enemies as impregnable. The landing will be made good, by the help of God and the Navy. The positions will be stormed and the war brought one step nearer to a glorious close. 'Remember', said Lord Kitchener, when bidding adieu to your commander, 'Remember, once you set foot upon the Gallipoli Peninsula you must fight the thing through to a finish.'

In turn, Hunter-Weston issued special orders for the 29th Division. He told his men to expect 'heavy losses by bullets, by shells, by mines and by drowning.' This depressing information could not have given his men much confidence, but Hunter-Weston was at least being realistic.

At dawn on 25 April the Australians and New Zealanders went ashore at Anzac Cove and gamely clawed their way into the steep hills only a few hundred yards inland. The beach landings at Helles were much more bloody. At V Beach the *River Clyde* disgorged men of the Munster Regiment and Hampshire Regiment, straight into concentrated Turkish small-arms fire. Only a few men reached the beach. The Dublin Fusiliers, coming ashore in ships' boats, were slaughtered in their hundreds. Hunter-Weston, on board HMS *Euryalus*, could hear the firing at V Beach but did not ask to be taken there to see what was happening. At 8.30 a.m., 2 hours after the beginning of the carnage, he gave the order for the main body to land from the ships. There was more carnage.

The flagship and Hamilton's battle HQ, HMS *Queen Elizabeth*, was off V Beach and Hamilton could clearly see what was happening. The ship's guns opened fire on the Turkish positions but when the bombardment ceased the surviving Turks returned to their posts and again prevented the pinned-down British troops from advancing. Hamilton considered diverting the other troops destined for the deadly V Beach to Y Beach, but was worried about the propriety of interfering with Hunter-Weston's operation. Instead of giving Hunter-Weston an order Hamilton sent him a question. 'Would you like to get some men ashore on Y Beach? If so, trawlers are available.' Hunter-Weston rejected the idea.

Hamilton believed that he was more accessible to his subordinates than any commander of a major force in history, and claimed that he was no more than 45 minutes away from any battle front. From his position of vantage on a ship he could see, sometimes with the naked eye, situations and crises not visible to the divisional generals on land.

All this being so he should have exercised more direct control, even taking over when necessary. By not doing so he was guilty of serious bungling. He gave only one order during the day of the landing and that to the Anzac leaders. It was a sound enough order but by the time it reached Birdwood's HQ he and his staff had already decided on the course of action which Hamilton had ordered.

His indecision at Helles on that first day was largely responsible for the failure of the campaign. Had he taken direct command it is almost certain that the British troops would have been in key positions before the Turkish reinforcements arrived. His vacillation continued next day, 26 April. That morning Hunter-Weston was told that the situation on Y Beach was desperate. This beach was directly under his command but he merely passed the message to Hamilton, saying that he had no reserves to spare. This was untrue; he had at least six battalions of French troops. Hunter-Weston had no grasp of the significance of the Y Beach operation. Hamilton did understand and was worried about it, but military etiquette was more important than making a decision. Still he did not take direct command; still he did not appoint another local commander.

At 9.30 a.m. *Queen Elizabeth* reached Y Beach. Hamilton could not find out precisely what was happening, but he saw soldiers descending the cliffs to the beach, where groups of other men stood around. 'I mistrusted and disliked the look of those aimless dawdlers by the sea,' he wrote. Here was reason enough for any Commander-in-Chief to be incisive. 'To see a part of my scheme, from which I had hoped so much, going wrong before my eyes is maddening,' he wrote. It was obvious to him that Hunter-Weston had divorced himself from Y Beach but still Hamilton took no action as Commander-in-Chief.

When he did make a decision – in relation to another part of the operation – he made the wrong one. The panicky and incompetent d'Amade wanted to evacuate his French troops from the Kum Kale position because, he said, there was no point in remaining there. Hamilton's chief-of-staff, Major-General W. Braithwaite, urged Hamilton to order d'Amade to hold firm and was backed by Admiral de Robeck, whose naval patrols were bringing in sound intelligence. Nevertheless Hamilton authorised the evacuation. A few hours later he heard that the Kum Kale operation had been a great success. The French had killed or wounded 1,700 Turks and had taken 500 prisoners for 800 casualties of their own. Hamilton withdrew his permission for d'Amade to evacuate – too late. That day his bungling did much to ensure that the campaign would fail.

At Helles, Hunter-Weston ordered, 'Every man will die at his post rather than retire.' In fact, the Turks were too weak to consider an assault and withdrew to a new line at Krithia which Hunter-Weston attacked at 8 a.m. on 28 April. His vague orders, which arrived too late at battalion level, resulted in lack of purpose and cohesion. Steadily losing control over his units and the course of the battle, Hunter-Weston ordered a withdrawal.

During this battle, Hamilton, who observed it, did what he should have done days before. He sent ashore one of his aides, the efficient Colonel C.F. Aspinall, to collect the scattered British soliders and lead them up the cliffs to their original positions. Aspinall steadied the front at that point.

Between dawn on 25 April and sunset on 28 April, Hamilton had lost 150 officers and 2,500 men killed, and another 250 officers and 6,000 men wounded. Nearly all the rest were exhausted. Yet he sent this despatch to Kitchener, 'Thanks to the weather and the wonderfully fine spirit of our troops all continues to go well.'

This was untrue but Hamilton, afraid of Kitchener, dared not tell him the truth. On the night of 30 April he told another untruth, this time to himself and his diary. Having came across a big batch of wounded, Hamilton wrote, 'I spoke to them and although some were terribly mutilated and disfigured, and although a few others were clearly dying, one and all kept a stiff upper lip – and all were, or managed to appear – more than content – happy! This scene brought tears to my eyes. The supreme courage of our soldiers! Were it not so, it would be unbearable.' In plain truth, the suffering men were anything but happy – except about leaving this 'hell heaped-up', as one of them called Gallipoli.

Following a major Turkish attack on the British lines at Helles, Hamilton initiated 'contentment and happiness' for more British soldiers by building up a force of 25,000 for Hunter-Weston to make a counter-attack. It was a formidable body of men, with a brigade of Australians and another of New Zealanders brought down the coast from Anzac sector, and a brigade of the excellent British 42nd Division from Egypt. Also, there were Gurkhas and Sikhs and 20 Australian field guns.

Hamilton told Hunter-Weston that he wanted him to attack before dawn on 6 May. 'It would be good tactics', he advised Hunter-Weston, 'to cross the danger zone by night and overthrow the enemy in the grey dawn.'

Good tactics indeed, but Hunter-Weston opposed them. He said that without enough trained officers an advance in the dark was unwise. In allowing his subordinate to have his way, Hamilton bungled again. He was allowing Hunter-Weston to make a frontal attack against a stubborn enemy in broad daylight. It cannot be said that Hunter-Weston organised his attack, he merely cobbled it together. No commander, senior or junior, knew precisely what their general required. Some did not understand that they were taking part in a major assault, others reached their jumping-off positions in the dark and the men hardly knew in what direction they were supposed to attack. Some unit HQs received their orders several hours after the assault began.

Hunter-Weston's plans – in so far as they can be called plans – could not have been more calculated to achieve his own defeat. He timed his attack for 11 a.m., thus giving the Turks plenty of time to have breakfast and organise themselves for the day. He had not sent out scouts by night to locate the enemy's trenches. He was attacking on a narrow front – 3 miles – without any feint or deception, oblique or flank attack. In addition – not his fault – he was short of shells. Not surprisingly, by the end of 6 May Hunter-Weston's exhausted troops had made no progress.

That night Hamilton wrote, 'We are now on our last legs. The beautiful battalions of 25 April are wasted skeletons. The thought of the river of blood against which I painfully made my way when I met these multitudes of wounded coming down to the shore was unnerving. To over-drive the willingest troops any general ever had under his command is a sin – but we go on fighting tomorrow.'

The multitudes of wounded belonged to Hunter-Weston, who was also in charge of the attack on 7 May. He made just one change in his plans; he jumped off at 10 a.m. instead of 11 a.m. His courageous men captured a few yards of ground here and there and as night fell sank exhausted to the ground.

Hunter-Weston was undismayed. For 8 May he ordered a third attack and this time Hamilton came ashore with his staff to observe the action. Hunter-Weston had a splendid spearhead force – 2,493 New Zealanders of the Otago, Wellington, Auckland and Canterbury battalions, under Colonel F.E. Johnstone. Their objective was held by about 8,000 Turks, most of their machine-guns still intact. Hunter-Weston's repeated attacks had practised the Turks nicely and when the New Zealanders, with the British 29th Division, went into the attack the Turks repulsed the survivors. It was all over by lunchtime. The French should have taken part in the assault but they did not leave the protection of their own lines. Their officers thought that Hunter-Weston was mad.

Hunter-Weston, brushing aside the vehement objections of Colonel Johnstone, ordered a fourth attack. Hamilton, being on the spot, could now hardly fail to become involved. Despite advice from some of his staff that Hunter-Weston's men were spent, Hamilton wanted another attack. Failure now, he reasoned, would be disastrous for morale. He discovered that three brigades, including the Australian 2nd Brigade, had not yet been used.

The next order came from the Commander-in-Chief, not from Hunter-Weston. The guns would pound the Turkish lines and then the whole Allied line would fix bayonets and storm the Krithia Line. The Australian 2nd Brigade's four Victorian battalions were to capture Krithia Spur, an exposed position. Hamilton sent a message that he wished all the infantry to make 'as much use of the bayonet as possible.'

Snatched from their uneaten evening meal, the Australians made an amazing uphill charge to capture and hold 1,000 yards of enemy territory, but it cost them more than one man in three killed or wounded. The brigade jumped off with 2,900 and suffered 1,056 casualties, including 16 officers killed and 32 wounded. Having lost 6,000 men in all on the night of 8 May, Hamilton and Hunter-Weston called off the battle. The badly wounded men suffered agonies before they were brought in and Chaplain O. Creighton of the 29th Division wrote, 'What a terrible waste it all seemed of such magnificent men.'[1]

Hunter-Weston's failure – which verged on the willfully negligent – did him no professional harm. On 24 May he was promoted to Lieut.-General and given command of the new VIII Corps, made up of all the British units at Helles. Then, on 4 June, he was allowed to fight the third battle of Krithia. About 30,000 British and French troops were used and by midday they had captured three successive lines of Turkish trenches – only to lose them again. The Collingwood Battalion of the Royal Naval Division was wiped-out. Of the 70 officers in the Howe and Hood Battalions 60 became casualties, as well as more than 1,000 of the 1,900 men who went into action.

Many British wounded perished between the opposing lines after major fighting. The Turks were usually willing to have an armistice to collect the wounded and bury the dead and made such arrangements with the Australians in the hills above Anzac Cove. The Turks asked for such a cease-fire after the British attacks at Krithia in June. Hunter-Weston – perhaps with GHQ's compliance – refused, apparently because he feared that the Turks might gain some advantage, though this was highly unlikely. So mutilated men lay in agony and parched with thirst in No-Man's-Land and sooner or later they died.

In a concise condemnation of the Helles butchery John North's 1936 comment remains unequalled. 'To the last, Helles conformed to a singularly brainless and suicidal type of warfare.'[2]

With the Anzacs steadily holding the central sector and Hunter-Weston steadily losing more men in the south, Kitchener sent Hamilton three New Army divisons for a new initiative in the north, at Sulva Bay. To command the new Corps Kitchener chose Lieut.-General Sir Frederick Stopford, with whom he sent a verbal message to Hamilton. The only way to make a real success of an attack was by surprise, he said, and assaulting prepared positions by daylight was a futile waste. The advice was months too late.

General Stopford had served as an ADC in Egypt and the Sudan in the 1880s and had been military secretary to General Redvers Buller early in the Boer War. He had retired in 1909 but was brought back into service when the army expanded so greatly in 1914–15. Stopford was only sixty-one but was in poor health – yet Kitchener sent him to fight a campaign in Gallipoli's appalling climate. Hamilton knew that Stopford had never commanded troops in battle and was aware of his various failings, yet gave him a free hand to plan the Suvla operations.

The task was simple enough. To give the Anzacs a chance of breaking through the enemy positions in the hills, Stopford had 22 fresh British battalions – 22,000 men – for an attack on the lowlands of Suvla Bay. He was required to capture low hills from 2 to 5 miles inland, at that time not occupied by the Turks, and opposing him were only 1,500 enemy troops. The experienced Birdwood guided and advised in every way he could. He even tactfully offered Stopford the elements of a battle plan – but Stopford ignored it.

Stopford read Hamilton's orders and from them he understood that all he had to do was land his Corps. This was a misunderstanding. Hamilton's language was ambiguous, but Stopford must have realised that merely putting his troops ashore would achieve nothing. Also, Birdwood and Hamilton had verbally made clear what was wanted of him.

On 3 August, with battle only 4 days off, Stopford sent Hamilton a message. 'I fear that it is likely that the attainment of security of Suvla Bay will so absorb the force under my command as to render it improbable that I shall be able to give direct assistance to the GOC Anzac in his attack on Hill 305.'

This should have alarmed Hamilton out of his chair and his staff into instant action, for Stopford was showing that he did not understand his assignment. But Hamilton was so unworried that he even allowed Stopford to make changes to the landing scheme.

The first brigades landed unopposed on the night of 6 August but did not move inland. More and more units landed, milled around and became hopelessly mixed. Only a few hundred yards away Stopford relaxed in his sloop, HMS *Jonquil*, while Hamilton waited for news on Imbros Island, 20 miles away. As General J.F.C. Fuller puts it, 'Both generals waited for victory or defeat as if the whole operation was a horse race. Such generalship defies definition.'[3]

Had Hamilton rushed to Suvla on a destroyer and insisted on an immediate advance into the hills, the official historian says, 'the duration of the world war might have been very considerably shortened.'[4]

As a result of Stopford's bungling the entire military plan collapsed and because of this, the naval supply plan as well. Indiscipline was rife, yet Stopford sent messages to two of his divisional commanders congratulating them on their achievements. They had achieved nothing whatever but Stopford seemed to think that he was not being a real Corps Commander unless he handed out praise. Stopford even fooled Hamilton into believing that his force was achieving great things, yet on most parts of his front all was quiet. On the coast a picnic-like atmosphere prevailed, with parties of men bathing.

Hamilton was finally alarmed enough to go to Suvla, where he found that chaos reigned. He left Stopford lounging on his sloop and with his aide went more than 2 miles inland, where he encountered Lieut.-General Sir Bryan Mahon, GOC 10th Division. He knew what Mahon should be doing but gave him no orders because, in Hamilton's view, etiquette demanded that he speak to Stopford first. Since Stopford had virtually abandoned command of the Corps, Hamilton's attitude becomes ridiculous.

Finally, the desperate Hamilton suggested to Kitchener that Stopford should be relieved and received permission to replace him with Major-General de Lisle. In his 9 disastrous days as GOC IX Corps Stopford had finally ensured that the campaign could not succeed. General Mahon then contributed to the debacle by refusing to serve under de Lisle, whom he detested.

Prime Minister Asquith regarded the Suvla Bay fiasco as his worst disappointment of the war. He wrote to Kitchener on 20 August, 'I have read enough to satisfy me that the generals and staff engaged in the Suvla part of the business ought to be court-martialled and dismissed from the army.' Hamilton himself lasted until 14 October, when the Dardanelles Committee ordered his recall.

The Anzacs were evacuated over a period of a week, the last men leaving on the night of 19–20 December. The garrison of Suvla departed at the same time. Helles was abandoned on the night of 9–10 January 1916. Because of magnificent staff work the men were away before the Turks discovered they had gone. An evacuation, no matter how brilliantly conducted, does not constitute a victory and nothing was achieved to compensate for the loss of 43,000 British and Empire dead.

It is possible to feel sorry for Hamilton. Kitchener handed him a difficult assignment without the time to prepare for it. He asked for a younger vigorous general to handle the Suvla operations and Kitchener gave him Stopford. He was let down by the French. His best troops, the Anzacs, were landed at the wrong place on Gallipoli's coastline. But none of these problems justified his almost wilful refusal to act the part of a Commander-in-Chief.

Few commanders in history have had it in their power to win a battle and possibly an entire campaign with a quick on-the-spot decision. Hamilton had that chance at Y Beach on the morning of 26 April. John North observed 21 years later, 'It must be another eternal regret of history that General Ian Hamilton did not yield to his natural inclination to get nearer the smoke of battle.'

Because Hamilton bungled his command Hunter-Weston and Stopford were allowed to bungle theirs. Llewellyn Woodward says of Stopford: 'He dallied and muddled, wasted invaluable time and thus allowed the Turkish reinforcements, which he could easily have forestalled, to reach the key positions first. No single act of incompetence had such far-reaching effects on the history of the war.'

Stopford disappeared from the war's stage. Hunter-Weston somehow left Gallipoli with his reputation intact and went on to bungle his part of the 1916 Somme campaign and thus cause the death of many of his own soldiers. It should be noted that at Helles this general awarded the Military Cross to a young officer who had summarily executed three men for alleged cowardice on the battlefield. That is, the general equated these executions with outstanding gallantry in the face of the enemy, for which the MC is usually awarded. To bestow an MC on this occasion was an insult to the decoration, to the dead soldiers and to the young officer himself.

NOTES

The Australian Official History of the Gallipoli campaign by C.E.W. Bean and the British Official History by C.F. Aspinall provide base material for a study of the campaign. Both authors were on the spot throughout. Hamilton's *Gallipoli Diary*, 1920, reveals much of the personality of the author and of his reactions to events.

1. Oliver Creighton, *With the 29th Division in Gallipoli*, 1916. He was killed in France in 1918.
2. John North, *Gallipoli: The Fading Vision*, Faber, 1936.
3. Major General J.F.C. Fuller, *The Decisive Battles of the Western World*, Vol III, Eyre & Spottiswoode, 1957.
4. C.F. Aspinall. He was the colonel sent ashore by Hamilton on 28 April to round up and command leaderless troops.
5. North, op cit.

TOWNSHEND
OF KUT

'Futile, Expensive Disaster'

N. DIXON, THE PSYCHOLOGY OF MILITARY INCOMPETENCE

Soon after the outbreak of the war in 1914 the British Government pressured the Indian Government into sending a small force to protect British oil interests in Mesopotamia, now Iraq. When Turkey entered the war on Germany's side the threat to the Ahwaz–Abadan pipeline became acute and the British Mesopotamia force was increased to divisional strength. The military men concerned with this force were the Commander-in-Chief India, Sir Beauchamp Duff, the GOC Mesopotamia, General Sir John Nixon, and the GOC Expeditionary Force D, Major-General Sir Charles Townshend. Between them they produced a military disaster described by one writer as 'so total yet unnecessary, so futile yet expensive, that its like did not occur again until the fall of Singapore in 1942.'[1]

The British Government's objective was straightforward. The Army must protect the oil refinery at Abadan and the pipeline to the coast. Nixon, who was as ambitious as he was stupid, wanted to do much more than this. He proposed to capture Baghdad. This was pure fantasy in a vast country with hostile terrain and climate, a large Turkish army and ruthless tribes who saw rich pickings in the vulnerable British force. Duff, who knew nothing whatsoever about conditions in Mesopotamia, aided and abetted Nixon.

The job of protecting the oil installations was relatively easy for the force supplied. The port of Basra, which the British and Indian troops occupied on 22 November 1914, was only 30 miles from Abadan and the transport required to cover this distance was adequate. Beyond Basra everything became more difficult because no road existed. All supply transport was by the Tigris river, which was full of shoals and sandbanks and bordered by marshes. It was not exactly a reliable line of communication.

Under Nixon, the British–Indian force pushed up both rivers to capture Amara, 100 miles north on the Tigris, on 3 June 1915. Townshend also took Nasiriya, a similar distance north on the Euphrates, on 25 July. The victories went to Nixon's head, the prize of Baghdad loomed large again and he decided to send a reinforced division northwards towards Baghdad. This was Townshend's force, largely the 6th Indian Division.

Townshend wrote to General Sir James Wolf Murray in England:

> I believe I am to advance from Amara to Kut-el-Amara. The question is where are we going to stop in Mesopotamia? We have certainly got enough good troops to make certain of taking Baghdad. I consider that we ought to hold what we have got as long as we are held up, as in the Dardanelles. All these offensive operations in secondary theatres are dreadful errors in strategy: the Dardanelles, Egypt, Mesopotamia, East Africa – I wonder and wonder at such expeditions being permitted in violation of all the great fundamental principles of war, especially that of Economy of Force. Such violation is always punished in history.
>
> I am afraid we are in the cold out here. The Mesopotamia operations are little noticed, though we are fighting the same enemy as in the Dardanelles, plus an appalling heat. The hardships in France are nothing to that.
>
> I have received great praise and have established a record in the way of pursuits.[2]

This letter showed an understanding of strategic essentials but Townshend behaved contrary to these essentials. Two weeks after writing to Murray he accepted without demur Nixon's order to advance 90 miles further to Kut and planned, on his own initiative, to pursue the Turks another 190 miles to Ctesiphon and

Kut-el-Amara, Mesopotamia

on to Baghdad. He was embarking on a major aggressive campaign with only the men and material for a minor defensive operation.

Impressively enough, Townshend defeated General Nureddin (or Nur-ud-din) at Kut but the Turkish army slipped away. Also, Townshend had suffered 12 per cent casualties instead of the 6 per cent he had allowed for. Under appalling conditions, many of the wounded died on unsprung supply carts, on filthy river barges and at the hands of marauding tribes.

Meanwhile Nixon and Beauchamp Duff – far away in Simla, India – irresponsibly encouraged Townshend to press on. Townshend was neither as stupid nor as ignorant as his superiors, but he was even more ambitious. Vain, egocentric and suffused with an almost Gallic desire for *la gloire*, he was already seeing himself as the uncrowned King of Baghdad. Pathetically ill-equipped for the task ahead, he marched his 14,000 troops ever onward.

At Ctesiphon, 20 miles from Baghdad, General Nureddin had entrenched a large army across the British line of advance.

Townshend was outnumbered by three to one – and knew this – but, on 22 November, he ordered an attack every bit as reckless as those taking place on the Western Front. His army was sharply repulsed, suffering 4,500 casualties. Having evacuated his wounded and sick back to Kut, Townshend himself fell back there on 2 December. General Nixon, at last apprehensive that he had incited Townshend to go too far, hastily withdrew himself and his staff to the safety of Basra.

Kut was a collection of mudhuts on a small tongue of land formed by a U-turn in the Tigris, and it was indefensible. Townshend had plenty of time to retreat to the safety of Amara and his men were fit enough. But he was more interested in his grand ambition than in the welfare of his men. Self indulgently, he decided to hold out in Kut, 'gallantly' awaiting relief by fresh troops from England, and again to advance on Baghdad. Fond of quoting from Hannibal, Wellington and Napoleon – and identifying with them according to the situation – Townshend regarded himself as a master of strategy. But he now disobeyed a fundamental maxim – 'Movement is the law of strategy'. He became immobile.

He sent a message to Nixon that he had only a month's supply of food for his British troops and urged rapid relief. This was a lie, for he had not yet attempted to ration his British or Indian troops. Kut was stuffed with hoards of Arab grain but Townshend gave no orders for it to be unearthed.

Nixon was frantic, for the setback would damage his own reputation. He needed time to prepare a relief column but his own panic and Townshend's importunacy induced him, prematurely, to send a column under Lieut.-General Fenton Aylmer. Struggling against floods and determined Turkish opposition, Aylmer lost 6,000 men between 18–21 January 1916 and turned back.

Supplies were being so mismanaged in Basra, and Nixon was so inefficient, that the Indian Government sent him a harbour expert, Sir George Buchanan, to break the impasse. This gave Nixon an opportunity to show the depth of his stupidity. He needed no help from experts, he said, and put obstacles in the way of Buchanan. Ships waited 3 weeks before being unloaded, just so that Nixon could show Buchanan who was boss. The disgusted Buchanan returned to India, where he reported that the whole supply arrangement in Basra was primitive and that the main dumps were located in a swamp.

Nixon urged Aylmer to make another attempt at relief, though Aylmer knew he was not strong enough. A capable general nevertheless, he sent messages to Townshend to ask for his co-operation. Aylmer reasoned that if Townshend arranged diversionary sorties from within Kut simultaneously with his own attacks, the relief force had a good chance of breaking through. Townshend refused. The master strategist was an advocate of feints, but now he said that since every feint he made from Kut must end in withdrawal it would be bad for morale. Morale was already bad enough and the smallest indication that relief was possible would have sent it soaring, but Townshend was obdurate. Aylmer had to do the job.

The unhappy but determined Aylmer did his best alone, however, on 8 March suffered 3,500 casualties and was repulsed. Meanwhile Nixon had been feeding false information to India and Britain, most infamously about the efficiency of the medical services. Expeditionary Force D had set off 17 medical officers and 50 assistants under strength, but Nixon did not disclose this. Wounded were due in Basra and from the British Government came a cable:

ON ARRIVAL WOUNDED BASRA PLEASE TELEGRAPH URGENT PARTICULARS AND PROGRESS.

Nixon replied:

MANY LIKELY TO RECOVER. MEDICAL SERVICES UNDER CIRCUMSTANCES OF CONSIDERABLE DIFFICULTY WORKED SPLENDIDLY.

Just before he sent this cable Nixon had seen the arrival of 600 casualties on two lighters towed by the armed river steamer

Mejidieh. For nearly 2 weeks wounded men had lain in pools of blood, urine, vomit and excreta. Covered in sores and crawling with maggots, they were suffering from untreated wounds caused by bullets and shells. Many were starving, nearly dead from thirst, and delirious.

Townshend was also lying. He consistently reported that he had food 'for only a few days'. Because of this he was urged from Basra to break out rather than starve. Townshend then reported that his officers had 'suddenly discovered' food for 56 days and, later, for 84 days. He was also lying about the strength of the enemy between himself and Aylmer. His Intelligence was good but he deliberately under-estimated the number of enemy to induce Aylmer to attack. Townshend had no intention of breaking out. In terms of glory and reward, the next best thing to the capture of Baghdad was the gallant holding of a beleaguered outpost surrounded by hordes of enemy.

Throughout the siege Townshend behaved in an extraordinary way for a man responsible for 12,000 loyal troops, who thought of him as 'Our Charlie'. He kept his signal staff on duty day and night tapping out in Morse code trivial messages to his friends in London. At least three times he asked for promotion to lieut.-general. Twice he suggested that he, alone, should escape from Kut because his leadership might well be needed elsewhere. Three times he suggested to Basra that GHQ should negotiate the exchange of Kut and its guns for the release of himself and his men. But this student of military history knew very well that on such occasions the enemy only allow the commander to go free. He even tried to curry favour with General Nureddin by sending him sycophantic letters. The great majority of the British soldiers, reduced by March to 2,000 in number, and the 8,000 Indians, knew nothing of all this. Not a single ordinary soldier was ever allowed to send a signals message to his family at home.

Late in March Nixon was at last removed from command at Basra, to be succeeded by General Sir Percy Lake. Lake sent yet another relief force up the river, this time commanded by George Gorringe, a friend of Townshend. From the signal which Townshend received he heard that Gorringe had been promoted lieut.-general – and burst into tears on a subaltern's shoulder. Since Gorringe was his junior in service he realised that he himself had been passed over for promotion.

Gorringe did as well as could be expected. His relief force broke through the first Turkish line but, on 22 April, it was pushed back. By now 23,000 men had been killed or wounded in various attempts to rescue a garrison of less than half that number, whose own commander could easily have brought them out earlier. Townshend sent no signal of thanks for the efforts made to relieve Kut, or of regret for the losses.

Food finally did, genuinely, run out. It had lasted 147 days, rather longer than Townshend's estimated 'month at most'. On 29 March 1916 Townshend surrendered. His correspondence with Nureddin had been worthwhile. He was received with effusive courtesy. Townshend even induced the Turkish commander to return his pet dog, Spot, safely to Basra.

With an adequate personal staff Townshend was transported in style to Baghdad and then on to Constantinople where he lived a fabulous life as the personal guest of the Turkish Commander-in-Chief, Mustafa Kemal, the victor of Gallipoli.

A lucky 345 prisoners were exchanged for an equal number of Turkish prisoners. Sir Beauchamp Duff ordered that the released men must not talk in public about the suffering of those they had left behind.

The Turks were brutal with the rest of the men of Expeditionary Force D. Under the whips of their Kurdish guards, they set off on a 1,200-mile march across fearsome country and in their thousands they died of starvation, dysentery, cholera, typhus, freezing cold, great heat and exhaustion. They could drop out of the column if they wished – only to be attacked by tribesmen who filled their mouths with sand and left them to die. Seventy per cent of the British troops and 50 per cent of the Indian soldiers died in captivity.

Only one senior officer, to his great credit, insisted on marching into captivity with the men. He was Major-General Mellia, a hard-fighting, rough-and-tumble commander with a personality so forceful that he often bullied the Turks into improving conditions for their captives.

When he returned home at the end of the war, Townshend made a speech, during which he cheerfully referred to himself as having been 'the honoured guest of the Turks'. He never did understand that this would seem offensive to the relatives of the 7,000 men of the Kut garrison who had died in captivity.

Professor Norman Dixon, who has studied Townshend, Nixon and Beauchamp Duff from a psychological standpoint, considers that they had something in common with the Nazi war criminal Eichmann and others of his kind, who were also able to carry out their job without apparently experiencing guilt or compassion. He finds that the Kut disaster trio were 'devoid of a sentiment which most people experience.' Townshend, Dixon says, was a disturbed personality, with a fatal flaw under an agreeable veneer. He likens him to Hermann Goering.

It is not necessary to exercise the judgment of hindsight to assess Townshend as a general. Failure to understand the limitations of weapons was, in his case, not a factor. It was not a matter of using the wrong tactics against modern weapons for the Turks were no better armed than Townshend's division. Townshend can be allowed none of the excuses sometimes made for the bunglers of the Western Front, because he had shown that he was capable of brilliant generalship. He was a gratuitous bungler, a calculating man who made his decisions deliberately. He was not a congential liar but a tactical one.

Much more intelligent than his superior, Nixon, Townshend must have known that by cooping himself up in Kut he was sacrificing his men. He knew that the Turks would show no mercy. While he butchered fewer of his own men than the generals on the Western Front, in a way he was worse than they were because of the cold-blooded deliberation with which he acted.

With the fall of Kut, British defeat and humiliation in Mesopotamia was complete. New life was instilled into the British forces there with the arrival, in August 1916, of General Sir Frederick Maude, a fine commander in every sense. Building up his manpower and supplies, he launched a fresh British–Indian offensive up the Tigris on 13 December 1916. Advancing methodically with almost 50,000 men, he spent 2 months eliminating the Turkish detachments south of the river. On 17 February he began a series of well-planned strikes against Kut, which the Turks had turned into a fortress with a garrison of 12,000 troops under General Kara Bekr Bey. Only 8 days later the Turks retreated.

Steadily fighting his way upriver, Maude reached the Turkish defences on the Diyala River, 10 miles below Baghdad, on 4 March. His skilful deployment forced the 11,000 Turks to abandon their lines without a fight. General Halil Pasha hurriedly withdrew north of Baghdad. Maude occupied it on 11 March, taking 9,000 prisoners.

Townshend had wanted to be 'The Man of Mesopotamia'. In reality Maude was that man.

NOTES

Two important biographies have been written about Townshend. They are *The Siege*, by Russell Braddon, Cape, London, 1969 and *Townshend of Kut*, by A.J. Barker, Cassell, 1967.
1.   Professor Norman Dixon, *The Psychology of Military Incompetence*, Cape, 1976. See Notes, Chapter 1.
2.   Quoted in Braddon's book.

6

HAIG
and the
SOMME

One Day, 20,000 Dead

Douglas ('Lucky') Haig, in complete control of operations on the Western Front since the middle of December 1915, believed that he had learnt the main lesson of 1915's battles. To achieve a breakthrough, the next great attack had to be much more thoroughly planned, much stronger and on a wider front than had been previously considered.

In the meantime, minor fighting continued so that the Germans would not get the idea that the Britsh and Empire armies were relaxing. Press correspondents were given ready access to the battlefields, especially if they were uncritical. A *Daily Mail* man, reporting on 18 February 1916, commented, 'If I were asked to tell the most extraordinary fact of life out here, in the trenches, I would say that it is the absence or fewness of new emotions of any kind and the rarity of fear.' It was mid-winter and the troops were too frozen to show emotions but in the trenches they lived in constant tension and fear.

Nevertheless, after the dreadful disasters under Sir John French, Haig gave the troops new hope for 1916. A young officer in Kitchener's New Army describes him as 'a wonderful looking man, with a very firm chin and dark blue eyes. He is rather short but very broad and strong looking. He looks at everything so directly and deliberately. He never takes his eyes off the eyes of the man he is talking to.' This is an interesting description since so few soldiers ever did see Haig.

Haig and his 300 staff officers at GHQ, situated at Montreuil, as well as the various Army HQ staffs, spent the first 6 months of 1916 preparing a breakthrough onslaught against the German lines. In collaboration with the French, it would take place in the Somme river region. The name Battle of the Somme has gone down in British history, but it was the French who would actually attack astride that river. The British effort was to push up the valleys and spurs leading up to the wide chalk ridge which the Germans occupied north of the Somme. This was Poziéres Ridge.

Haig proposed to use about 700,000 men, a seven to one superiority over the Germans on that sector. Included among his units would be the Australian divisions, which Haig knew would soon be leaving Egypt for Europe. His offensive, known to his staff as 'The Big Push', would surely end the war. It was destined to be the largest and longest continuous engagement fought since the beginning of recorded history.

During the British planning phase, in February the French army became massively committed to the defence of the fortress region of Verdun, where they were suffering heavy casualties. The British attack on the Somme would therefore become the main Allied effort of the period. A smaller French force would attack south of the river while the British attacked north of it.

Planning finished towards the end of June but long before that date preparations were in hand, all consistent with Haig's obsessive need for order. While confidence was the key word, careful calculations were nevertheless made to ascertain the number of men available for expenditure in casualties. The figure arrived at was 500,000.

Haig's principal senior co-planner was General Sir Henry Rawlinson, GOC 4th Army, whose men were to make the initial attack. Haig and Rawlinson were accustomed to thinking in threes. There were three land combat formations – artillery, infantry and cavalry – and they were seen as entirely distinct from one another. They operated to a set sequence. The artillery pounded away while the other two arms waited immobile. Then, as Haig and Rawlinson had planned it, the infantry took over and the other two became immobile. When the infantry had achieved its task of penetration it held fast while the cavalry went through the gaps in pursuit. This was how any decent battle should be fought. The pattern was so rigid that despite profound and bloody evidence on the Somme that it did not work it was not changed for 2 weeks.

Lieut.-General Sir Lancelot ('Kigg') Kiggell, Haig's Chief of General Staff, also believed in a four-row infantry attack and said so in a training memorandum which he issued only 3 weeks before the offensive began. In the same paper he warned, 'All must be prepared for heavy casualties.' He was ensuring heavy casualties with his tactics.

The tall, gangling Rawlinson – 'Rawly' to his friends – must bear much of the responsibility for the dreadful failure of the Somme offensive, and especially for the carnage on the first day. Any bright ideas or constructive suggestions made by his staff were brushed aside. He could no more brook criticism than could Haig, as is shown with blunt clarity in April 1916 in the Fourth Army's *Tactical Notes*, produced by Rawlinson's Chief-of-Staff, Major-General A.A. Montgomery. One passage in the 32-page document is stressed. It states, 'It must be remembered that all criticism by subordinates of their superiors, and of orders received from superior authority, will in the end recoil on the head of the critics and undermine their authority with those below them.' These might be Montgomery's words but they are Rawlinson's attitudes. The passage also shows Rawlinson's poor standard of logical thought, since it is not at all clear why junior officers' loyalty would be harmed by a senior criticising an officer who was even more senior.

Rawlinson's uncriticisable overconfidence influenced some of his divisional commanders. In April, 2 months before the Somme offensive, Major-General Ivor Maxse, GOC 18th Division, said that any general could 'take over the enemy's front line trenches without many casualties to ourselves. The artillery makes front

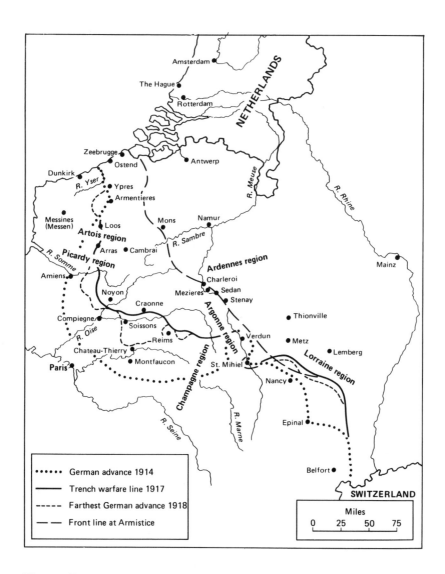

Western Front

line trenches easy prey to an attack.' This thinking was as unrealistic as that of Haig and Rawlinson, though it should be said that Maxse later learned from his mistakes and became a more enterprising general.

Rehearsals for the big assault were farcical. Acres of dusty ground were lined with tapes to represent trenches and the men then assaulted and 'captured' the tapes. Everything was done in the imagination. The soldiers were ordered to imagine gas, barbed wire and artillery fire. Men with flags were posted in front of the advancing waves to represent bursting British shells. The attackers were then told, 'Imagine that you are wearing full gear, and that you are carrying wire, bombs and pigeons.' And all the time there was an insistence on a steady walk. The Staff had convinced themselves that the troops would become confused if other tactics were employed – such as rushing from cover to cover, firing on the move or following close upon a creeping barrage from their own guns. This belief resulted from the idea, prevalent among British regulars, that the volunteers of Kitchener's army were very dull men. This was not so; many intelligent men had responded to the call for the New Army.

The rehearsals were carried out in silence, by numbers, and as a drill. Unrealistic and impractical, they gave the troops no sense of battle, merely the dangerously misleading impression that the initial assault would be a walkover.

With the backing of his senior staff officers, Rawlinson prescribed an assault by four rows of advancing infantry. He was prepared to admit that two or three rows sometimes succeeded in capturing enemy positions, but four rows was a much more certain method. It is not a matter of hindsight to say that, in effect, Rawlinson was planning to bring about heavy casualties among his own men. He was simply giving German machine-gun bullets a better target. His four-row advance was an almost incomparable tactical blunder.

Rawlinson issued instructions that advancing troops were not to charge, merely to walk. In any case, he told a conference of corps commanders, after the guns had done their job it was only necessary to stroll over and take possession of the German trenches.

A total of 1,537 guns would fire more or less continuously for 8 days before the infantry advance. The generals confidently anticipated that the explosions would cut the German barbed wire defences and obliterate the frontline positions. In the event, these guns fired 1,738,000 shells.

Despite Rawlinson's heavy reliance on artillery he had too few heavy guns. He used only one 6-inch howitzer per 45 yards compared with the French army's one per 20 yards. Shrapnel was used for cutting the enemy wire instead of high explosive shells. That high explosive was more effective is not the revelation of hindsight. It was obvious that steel shrapnel balls, the size of small marbles, could not cut wire as efficiently as large, jagged chunks of steel slicing through the air with tremendous velocity.

Haig took out a form of insurance by ordering his chaplain, Revd George Duncan, a priest of the Church of Scotland, to be present at his advanced HQ when the battle commenced. He had been impressed by one of Duncan's sermons on the subject of prayer in battle. The chaplain illustrated his message by the devotions of the Scottish troops at the Battle of Bannockburn in 1314 when the Scots had resoundingly beaten the English. 'With God's help', Haig was confident of success at the Somme despite His apparent absence at Loos. He wrote to his wife that every step in his plan had been taken with 'the Divine help'.

On 30 June, the eve of the great assault, Haig wrote: 'The men are in splendid spirits. Several have said that they have never before been so instructed and informed of the operation before them. The wire has never been so well cut, nor the artillery preparation so thorough. I have personally seen all the corps commanders and one and all are full of confidence.'

At that time Rawlinson knew that not all the wire had been cut and that the German trenches were looking in remarkably good shape despite the weight of British shells. That he did not complain about this or take the serious information to Haig proves him to be not only an incompetent but a moral coward. It has to be assumed that he dared not face Haig with unpalatable intelligence and certainly not so late in the day. Haig had decreed that the offensive would be unleashed and that it would be successful, so Rawlinson kept these late misgivings to himself and passed them on to nobody except his diary.

'What the actual result will be, none can say', Rawlinson wrote, 'but I feel pretty confident of success myself – that the Boche will break. That a débacle will supervene I do not believe, but should this be the case I am ready to take full advantage of it. The issues are in the hands of the Bon Dieu.'

The issue should never have been left in the hands of the Bon Dieu, though even without formal military training in the Royal Military Academy and the Staff College He might well have achieved better results than Rawlinson, especially as the Chaplain-General was sure He was on the British side. Nevertheless, Rawlinson, not B.D., was commanding Fourth Army. His confession that he did not know the outcome contradicted his earlier certainty that the troops only had to stroll across No-Man's-Land after the bombardment and occupy the German trenches.

An attack covered by the half-light of dawn had not been considered necessary so at 7.30 a.m. on the warm, sunny morning of 1 July the British guns lifted to more distant targets and the attacking waves of 11 British divisions climbed out of their trenches, on a 13-mile front, and walked forward.

By 7.31 a.m. the six German divisions facing them had carried their machine-guns upstairs from the safe and comfortable deep cellars and were spraying the attackers advancing in their orderly rows. A German machine-gunner wrote, 'We were surprised to see them walking, we had never seen that before. The officers went in front. I noticed one of them walking calmly, carrying a walking stick. When we started to fire we just had to load and reload. They went down in their hundreds. We didn't have to aim, we just fired into them.'

A German officer reported his impression of the attack. 'Whole sections appeared to fall. All along the line, Englishmen could be seen throwing their arms into the air and collapsing, never to move again. Badly wounded rolled about in agony, while other casualties crawled into shell holes for shelter. But the British soldier has no lack of courage. His lines, though badly

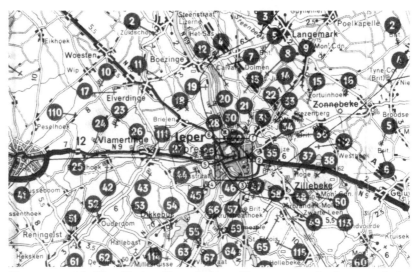

Commonwealth War Graves Commission military cemeteries in part of the Ypres Salient. Each dot marks a cemetery

shaken with many gaps, now came on faster. The noise of battle became indescribable.'

Swept by traversing machine-guns, stopped by uncut wire, the rigid, slow-moving lines were then enveloped by bursting German shells. To add to the hideous confusion, a British mine exploded late, causing heavy casualties in several advancing battalions. Wave after wave went down, horrifying those who followed them. In a few places groups of British were successful and clung to hard won positions while they waited for reinforcements. But they too had been massacred.

Two brigades of the 8th Division were mown down by German gunners around Ovillers. In 2 hours the division lost 218 of its 300 officers and 5,274 of its 8,500 other ranks. The German defenders lost 300 men. At Fricourt, two whole battalions, 10th West Yorkshires and 7th Green Howards, were virtually annihilated by one enemy Maxim machine-gun. At Y Ravine, near Beaumont Hamel, the Newfoundland Regiment was sent in against machine-gun fire; 710 men fell, practically the entire unit.

Henry Williamson, among the attackers at Ovillers, advanced with his men 'In the flame and rolling smoke I see men arising and walking forward; and I go forward with them, in a glassy delirium wherein some men seem to pause with bowed heads, and sink carefully to their knees, and roll slowly over, and lie still. Others roll and roll, and scream and grip my legs in uttermost fear, and I have to struggle to break away, while the dust and earth on my tunic changes from grey to red.'[1]

Brigadier-General E.L. Spears, Liaison Officer with the French, watched attacks by both armies. 'How enraging to think of the irreparable waste,' he wrote. 'A French artillery observation officer said to me, "I thought of the Crimea today, and of what the French said in the Crimea during the Charge of the Light Brigade." [C'est magnifique, mais ce n'est pas le guerre. This is magnificent but it is not war.]'[2]

Of the 110,000 men who attacked, 60,000 were killed or wounded on this one day. About 20,000 lay dead between the lines.

Haig himself must bear the responsibility for the miscalculation that the bombardment would destroy every German in the area covered by it. Even if this estimate had been accurate for the first line of German trenches it could not have applied to the second line. Rawlinson was more directly responsible because of his careless assumptions that the artillery would prepare the ground so that the infantry had only to walk in, that capturing the first line of enemy trenches was relatively simple and that consequently consolidation was more important than the assault.

Haig's chronicler, Colonel Boraston, writes that the attack 'bore out the conclusions of the British Higher Command, and amply justified the tactical methods employed.' This is an outrageous statement. It is more accurate to call 1 July 1916, as does H. L'Etang, 'probably the biggest disaster to British arms since Hastings. . . . Certainly never before, nor since, had such wanton, pointless carnage been seen, not even at Verdun, where in the worst month of all [June] the total French casualty list barely exceeded what Britian lost on her *one* day.'[3]

Writing in 1936, Lady Haig explained something of her husband's attitude to his losses. Apparently he was alarmed by the 'seemingly' heavy casualties until he learnt that they included a large proportion of lightly wounded.

The total casualties for the first 3 days approached 100,000. British casualties on the first day were 60,000. According to Lady Haig, in other armies men as lightly wounded as those in the British Army would not have left the field; presumably this information came from Haig himself.

German losses on 1 July are hard to estimate because daily casualty returns were not part of the German army procedure. The probable figure is 8,000, of whom 2,000 were prisoners.

Haig was bitter about the failure of the assault. As he saw the action, the 3rd Army's attack on the Gommecourt sector, though beaten off, had given a magnificent opportunity for VIII Corps. The GOC VIII Corps was none other than General Sir Aylmer Hunter-Weston, the butcher of Helles. Haig wrote: 'VIII Corps began well but as the day progressed were forced back. I am inclined to believe from further reports that few of the VIII Corps left their trenches.'

He should have known Hunter-Weston better. Whatever his deficiencies, Hunter-Weston was not the man to fail to push an attack. He had shown at Helles that his own heavy casualties did not deter him. It is worth examining the relationship between Haig and Hunter-Weston, Hunter-Weston's plans for his part of the opening day of the offensive, and what he did when they failed.

Haig had no great faith in Hunter-Weston even before 1 July and considered him and his officers to be amateurs. After all, they had only been fighting Turks and Haig had no respect whatever for the Turks as fighting men. He considered that the Gallipoli campaign had been lost by Hamilton's inept leadership, which was largely true. But the Turks were not the fanatical, ill-trained dervishes that Haig imagined them to be. Hunter-Weston had been a failure at Helles but he was hardly an amateur, in the sense in which Haig meant, after 8 months on the peninsula.

Hunter-Weston was confident that he could tactically handle artillery and the fire plan for 1 July was in his hands. He ordered the heavy artillery, which fired destructive high-explosive shells of large calibre, to lift off the enemy trenches 10 minutes before zero. The field artillery, firing 13- and 18-pounder shells with a mixture of high-explosive and shrapnel shells, was to stop 2 minutes before zero.

Many of his officers were appalled. They knew that the guns should keep firing at least until after the British infantry had left their trenches. In this way the men had a chance of reaching the enemy trenches before the enemy infantry manned them. Hunter-Weston, from his rear position and informed by nothing more reliable than his own fantasy, declared after the bombardment that the Germans' wire would be blown away and that the troops could safely walk in. In this he was obviously under the spell of his Army commander, Rawlinson, who preached the same gospel.

With ever greater certainty, on 1 July, Hunter-Weston's officers, from division down to brigade and brigade to battalion, reported that the wire had not been blown away. The company officers in the front jumping-off trench could see it standing, right along the front.

As planned, VIII Corps pushed off for its attack on Serre and Beamont Hamel, but made no progress. Haig did the men an injustice, for 14,000 of them lay dead, dying or wounded. Hunter-Weston's absurd artillery fire plan had finished them by leaving them exposed to German machine-gunners.

Even if Haig at that time did not know the full extent of VIII Corp's casualties, Hunter-Weston did. The very next day he moved to steer blame away from himself. Writing direct to the Chief of the Imperial General Staff personally, Robertson, he blamed the artillery for failing him. He complained that the guns had neither destroyed the German trenches nor the enemy guns. He could have done so much better had the British artillery supported him adequately. Anyway, he said, the British guns did not have enough shells, especially on his sector.

Gunnery officers were amongst the most professional of British army officers and many of their ideas were innovative and sensible. But they were obliged to give the infantry generals the sort of gunfire they asked for. In blaming the gunners Hunter-Weston was blaming himself. The artillery officers had tried to persuade Hunter-Weston to be more realistic in his fire plan and little fault lay with them, though they did not have enough guns for the task which Haig had set them.

Because of the confusion and the breakdown of communications, GHQ could not know the precise extent of the casualties at the end of 1 July, but Haig knew that night that he had suffered a loss of at least 40,000 men.

The casualties were even heavier than the High Command had allowed for. For instance, between Albert and Amiens a casualty clearing station had been established, with tented wards for an anticipated 1,000 patients on a particular sector during the offensive. It dealt with 10,000 in the first 48 hours. A surgeon wrote:

> Streams of ambulances a mile long waited to be unloaded. The whole area of the camp, a field of six acres, was completely covered with stretchers placed side by side, each with its suffering or dying man. We surgeons were hard at it in the operating theatre, a good hut holding four tables. Occasionally we made a brief look around to select from the thousands of patients those few we had time to save. It was terrible.

Haig appeared undismayed by the number of casualties and with the help of the London press – he had friends among the newspaper proprietors – he set about convincing Britian that all was going according to plan.

Lord Northcliffe's *The Times* on 3 July reported the first day's attack with a breezy confidence; after all, the Commander-in-Chief's word was not to be doubted. 'Sir Douglas Haig telephoned last night', said *The Times*, 'that the general situation was favourable.' The account coasts on smoothly to report 'effective progress, nay, substantial progress.' Changing up to top gear rhetoric, the account goes on: 'There is a fair field and no favour and we have elected to fight out our quarrel with the Germans and to give them as much battle as they want. . . . We got our first thrust well home, and there is every reason to be sanguine as to the result.'

At the time this nonsense was being printed many wounded British soldiers lying helpless on the battlefield were still crying out with pain.

The Observer commented, 'A grandeur of being beyond all that our country has known before is purchased for those who live by those who die. For Britain, these days are only at the beginning of what may come. The New Armies, fighting with a valour and fibre never surpassed by any people, have excelled our best hopes.'

Beach-Thomas of the *Daily Mail* reported that, 'The very attitudes of the dead, fallen eagerly forwards, have a look of expectant hope. You would say that they died with the light of victory in their eyes.'

On 4 July, 4 days after the commencement of the battle, the *Morning Post* brought reassurance to its readers.

> The seamy side of war, which it is impossible wholly to exclude from one's contemplation, has been rather painfully in evidence today. . . . While nothing is to be gained by disguising the fact that in a great military movement such as is now in progress, our losses must be considerable, I am glad to be able to report that as I hinted yesterday, that a large number of our casualties belong to the category of 'slightly wounded'. The cheeriness of our men, who, in their own language, have 'copped it', is beyond all praise. With frayed and tattered uniforms, splashed with blood, they think not of their wounds. 'Tell me', they say, 'how are we going on? Is everything all right?' And when they are told: 'Yes, quite all right,' they are more than content.

On 6 July the Special Correspondent of the *Morning Post* brought the British public words of comfort from army chaplains.

> Today our dead were being prepared for burial. Three chaplains, representing different religious denominations, were in readiness. 'My God', said one of them to me, 'how brave and devoted our dear soldier boys are. Look at them now where they lie – every man with his face to the foe. They never fear death. To them it is simply one of the fortunes of war.'

If the chaplain was correctly reported he was guilty of one of the most hideous perversions of language committed during the entire war. To call being killed in battle 'simply one of the fortunes of war' is monstrous, but the attitude could well reflect a similar cast of mind in some generals. Quite apart from the dishonesty of 'They never fear death', the statement shows a total failure to grasp reality. By the time the chaplains saw the corpses they would have been arranged in rows, ready for burial, face forwards – those who still had a face. The priests could not possibly have known which way the men faced as they died.

General Rawlinson was not as 'contented' as the *Morning Post* reported the wounded soldiers to be. He ordered his staff to recall and destroy the notes he had issued as a guidance for the attack. This could only have been because he realised that he had blundered, though it is impossible to calculate how many of his own soldiers he had killed and maimed as a result of his blunders. Later, members of Fourth Army staff removed the Army War Diary and substituted another version in an attempt to cover up Rawlinson's culpability on 1 July, and their own inadequacies.

It has been said that the British lost the Battle of the Somme by 3 minutes. Had the troops not been encumbered with so much weight of gear and had they been ordered to charge they would have been onto the German front positions before the enemy could man them. It was a calculation which had apparently not entered the minds of the planners.

Many battles in history had been called off after the loss of far fewer men than 60,000 in one day. Haig never entertained the idea of calling off the offensive. For political–psychological reasons he was forced to continue. To break off would be an open admission of failure. By continuing he could 'prove' that he never intended to breakthrough but that his strategy was a wearing-down battle of attrition. The offensive was only a few weeks old when the story was spread by officially inspired apologists that Haig was aiming thoughout at a campaign of attrition and had not dreamt of a breakthrough. Liddell Hart says, 'This denial was vehemently maintained for years, long after the war; it forms one of the most elaborate perversions of historical truth that has come to light. The "smoke screen", composed of particles of truth dishonestly mixed, was finally dissipated by the publication of the *Official History* in 1932.'[4]

The more obvious causes of that day's failure include:

The failure of 'Lucky' and 'Rawly' to integrate their respective plans.
Neglect of field intelligence – that is, from infantry patrols – which indicated that the Germans had virtually shellproof dugouts. Many were two storeys deep.
The refusal by Rawlinson to admit to himself that much of the German wire defences remained uncut on the night of 30 June.

A not so obvious cause is what I shall term the HCI Fixation – Heavy Casualties Inevitable. The general who works to this fixation automatically seals off the upper reaches of his brain. A pattern had been set in 1914 and during 1915 it had been firmly fixed. Heavy casualties were a basic rule of the game and simply had to be accepted. French worked to the HCI fixation and Haig followed it; most of their army and corps commanders simply copied them. The general who tolerates heavy casualties will assuredly get them, because he does not work at avoiding them.

Paul Fussell[5] says that the final cause of the 1 July disaster was the 'hopeless absence of cleverness about the whole thing, entirely characteristic of its author' [Haig]. Fussell had in mind the simple tactic of lifting the bombardment for 2 minutes at dawn – the expected hour for an infantry attack – and then immediately resuming it in the hope of trapping the German machine-gunners at their firing positions.

Fussell finds another cause for failure in the British class system and the assumptions that it sanctioned. For instance, the regular staff officers were contemptuous of the novices who made up the New Army, which was largely recruited from working men of the English Midlands. He believes that the Staff saw these men as 'too simple and animal' to cross No-Man's-Land in any way other than well aligned rows.

From 1 July 1916 Haig at the front and Robertson at home as Chief of the Imperial General Staff, set the course for the rest of the war. Both believed that victory could be won only on the Western Front and they knew no tactics other than frontal assaults.

HAIG AND THE SOMME

David Lloyd George and other men worried about the Haig–Robertson philosophy of war, and aware of the waste and futility of the Western Front campaigns, could muster little power against this formidable combination. As Minister of Munitions, Lloyd George did what he could to help the troops. It was he who ignored the High Command's resistance to the machine-gun and ordered an issue of 16 to each battalion. This was still too low a number but infinitely better than Haig's recommended 2 to a battalion.

It was also Lloyd George who overruled the generals' objections and brought the quick-firing light mortar into general use in the army. It developed into the war's outstanding trench weapon.

Haig had told a friend, after more than a year of trench warfare, that generals 'after a certain time of life are apt to be narrow-minded and disinclined to take advantage of modern scientific discoveries. The civilian minister can do good by pressing the development of some modern discovery.' Haig himself never encouraged any such pressing, especially from Lloyd George.

On 3 August Haig sent a despatch concerning 'The Principle on which we should act.' He wrote, 'Maintain our offensive. Our losses in July's fighting totalled about 120,000 more than they would have been had we not attacked. They cannot be regarded as sufficient to justify any anxiety as to our ability to continue the offensive.'

His rationalisation of losses is grotesque. How would the losses have been incurred had he not attacked? He never did explain.

In no way afflicted by anxiety, despite having set an historical record for casualties suffered, he set about attrition which, simply put, meant causing the German leaders more casualties than they inflicted upon him. The side with the fewer losses would have to win, or so the Haig theory ran.

BUTCHERS AND BUNGLERS

NOTES

Statements attributed to Haig and Rawlinson come from their respective diaries, memoirs and, in Rawlinson's case, from training manuals.

1. Henry Williamson, an infantry officer throughout the war, wrote some of the best books about it. This quotation is taken from his *The Wet Flanders Plain*, Beaumont Press, 1929.
2. Spears, as a liaison officer, was in a unique position to observe the Somme and other battles. One of his best-known books is *Liaison 1914*, 1930.
3. H. L'Etang, a modern writer, wrote *Fit to Lead* in 1980.
4. Captain Basil Liddell Hart, a trenchant critic of military incompetence, was writing in his book *The Real War 1914–1918*, Cassell, 1930.
5. Paul Fussell's book *The Great War and Modern Memory*, Oxford University Press, 1975, is one of the most brilliant analyses of the war. He shows how the consciousness of a whole society was altered by the war.

7

HAIG, HAKING and GOUGH

'Incompetence, Callousness and Vanity'

LIEUT. J.A. RAWS, AIF, LETTERS HOME

The British generals' objective was now to capture favourable ground for an attack on the German second line, along the Poziéres–Thiepval Ridge. To do this several fortress villages and large, thick woods, which were rapidly filling with German reinforcements, had to be captured.

On 2 July, fresh British troops entering the line saw the human ruin of the previous day. Private George Coppard[1] commented on the 'hundreds of dead, strung out like wreckage washed up on a high water mark. Quite as many died on the wire as on the ground, like fish caught in a net. Some looked as though they were praying.' Lieut. Graham Greenwell[2] wrote in a letter home, 'The Germans have plenty of machine-guns, which can hold up armies. You would despair of ever making a big advance, especially with cavalry, if you could see the way in which troops are mown down by these little devils.'

La Boiselle was captured on 7 July but the Germans in Mametz Wood held firm. After every failure the senior commanders began an almost frantic hunt to find scapegoats and if individuals could not readily be found to take the blame then a whole division would do.

An example of this concerns the 38th (Welsh) Division at Mametz Wood. Major-General Archibald Montgomery, Chief-of-Staff to Rawlinson, reported that the 38th 'had done nothing' during the attacks of 5–8 July. On the following day General Kiggell, Chief of the General Staff at GHQ, told Haig that the 38th had failed to take Mametz Wood with 'quite insignificant losses', and were unworthy of the traditions of the army. This was unfair, insulting and incorrect. When 38th Division left Mametz Wood on 12 July – having captured it – they had suffered 4,000 casualties, including 7 battalion commanders.

Rawlinson, as culpably ignorant as the others about what was happening in the woods and trenches, was still blaming 38th Division; they should have occupied Mametz Wood earlier. He had already sacked the divisional commander, Major-General Ivor Philipps, and commented that 'he should have been got rid of before'.

By 13 July Rawlinson was ready for an assault on the German second line. He planned a surprise attack, the natural military thing to do but one which had been ignored for more than 16 months. After a short bombardment, his troops would advance in darkness behind a creeping barrage. The objectives were the ruined village of Bazentin-le-petit and Delville Wood.

As the bombardment lifted at 3.20 a.m. on 14 July, 22,000 troops advanced rapidly and by 10 a.m. they had made a gap about 3 miles wide in the German trench system. It seemed to be time for the cavalry but the Indian lancers arrived too late to do more than crush the enemy outposts protecting High Wood. The battle became a brutal, slogging maul. In 6 days 2,500 South Africans were killed as they captured and then held Delville Wood at Longueval. It was an heroic but bloody achievement.

In her 1936 book, Lady Haig[3] – by then Countess Haig – reported that Haig regarded the push of 14 July as the army's best day of the war. Still, she admitted that her husband had come in for much criticism, some of it from generals whom Haig had sacked.

General Sir Richard Haking, a veteran of campaigns in Burma and South Africa, and GOC XI Corps, pushed through an idea to

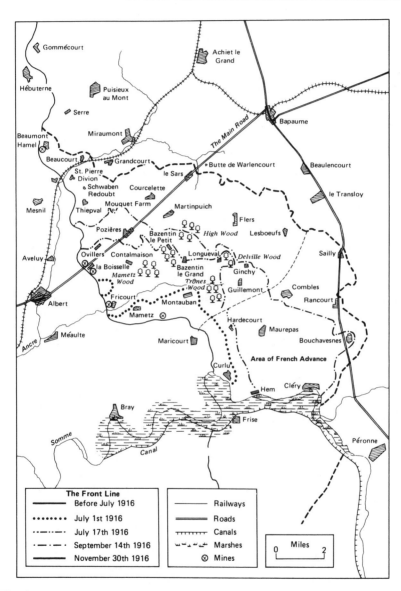

The Somme

capture the German positions between the village of Fromelles and Aubers Ridge. This battleground, known to British history as Fleurbaix but as Fromelles to the Australians, was 40 miles north of the Somme and the object of the attack was to prevent the German High Command from moving troops from the Lille area to the Somme. It would be a good plan, Haking argued, to tie them down with another British offensive.

Haking had always scorned the defensive and glorified the offensive. 'The offensive would win', he said, 'as sure as there is a sun in the heavens.' And this would apply even if the attacking force was weaker than the defenders. He did admit the attackers needed high morale but this could be achieved through good generalship. For Haking, a battle against the military enemy was as good as won when the 'enemy' within his own men had been vanquished. That enemy was human nature – the natural desire to defend rather than attack. Haking proposed to eradicate this desire from his men. He said as much in a book called *Company Training*, published in London in 1913. 'One often hears it stated that with modern weapons the defence has gained over the attack,' he wrote. 'If, however, it was possible to visit the front line of the attack and talk to the officers, NCOs and men, and then go over to the defenders' trenches and talk to them, one would discover several reasons why the attack is better than the defence.' The main reason, as perceived by Haking, was that the defenders feared the morale and therefore the invincibility of the attackers. All that worried Haking was that an ever increasing number of men came from urban areas, which he believed did not naturally produce good soldierly material.

Haking was a great advocate of trench raids. Often the raids which he ordered or encouraged had no particular purpose other than killing and destruction. To Haking war was a great adventure in which men needed to be blooded, rather in the way that foxhunting had the same ritual. Not only that, but raiding was good for morale. In this he was echoing Haig, though Haig may also have been echoing Haking. Senior commanders tended to support one another in such things – except when trying to find a scapegoat to cover up their own failures. The notion that trench

HAIG, HAKING AND GOUGH

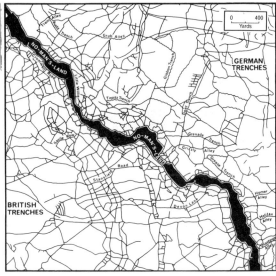

Trenches on the Western Front, 1917

raids raised morale was a fallacy, except perhaps in the case of the Australians who were peculiarly skillful in the art and highly successful. Most troops could accept raids with a definite purpose, such as capturing prisoners for interrogation, but raids which were carried out to indulge a general's whim were damaging to morale.

Haking had an obsession about Aubers Ridge. The British under Haig had twice lost heavily there in 1915 and Haking himself had suffered considerable loss in a similar attack in June 1916. Now Haking's plan was to soften up the Germans with a 3-day barrage, followed by an attack made by the British 61st Division and the Australian 5th Division, which had only recently come into the line.

The Australian Chief-of-Staff, Major-General Brudenell White, distrusted the plan, which he considered ill-prepared and hasty. He considered that Haking was heading for disaster and said so, but was over-ruled.

GOC First Army and Haking's immediate superior, General

Sir Charles Monro, decided to cancel the operation and in an urgent despatch he informed Haig of his decision. He received a firm negative:

> The Commander-in-Chief wishes the special operation to be carried out as soon as possible, weather permitting, providing always that General Monro is satisfied that the conditions are favourable, and that the resources at his disposal, including ammunition, are adequate both for the preparation and execution of the enterprise.

Now having been given free rein, Haking dictated that there must be no halt to seek cover; this would only cheer the defenders. The attack was to go in at 6 p.m. on 19 July, but the AIF 8th Brigade, waiting in their trenches, were heavily shelled before the men went over the top. No-Man's-Land here was 150–250 yards wide and German machine-gun fire was heavy. Despite their casualties, the 8th, 14th and 15th Brigades cleared the Germans from their trenches and following waves captured the support trenches. Soon the Australians were in the open country beyond the enemy positions.

Their stated objective was a third trench-line but they could not find it. It did not exist – Haking had made a mistake. After sheltering in ditches and shellholes the Australians made a rough line but the 14th Brigade's right flank was exposed. Haking ordered the 61st Division to attack at 9 p.m. to ease the pressure on the 14th. The depleted 15th also attacked, but only to discover, far too late, that the 61st's attack had been called off. In night-long hand-to-hand fighting the Germans worked their way round both flanks of the Australian position.

As the battle ended on the evening of 20 July the front line was filled with dead and dying. The AIF's official historian records that 'in front of the 15th Brigade the wounded could be seen everywhere raising their limbs in pain or turning hopelessly, hour after hour, from one side to the other.' In 27 hours the 5th Division lost 5,533 officers and men. The 60th Battalion went into the fight with 887 officers and men; only one officer and 106 men answered roll-call.

The tragedy at Fromelles was the result of muddled thinking. It was intended as a feint to keep German reserves away from the Somme battlefield. If the preparations for it, intentionally made obvious to the Germans, had lasted longer they might have achieved this object. But to do this the attack should not have been actually launched. Within a few hours of its launching the fact that it was only a feint was inevitably known to the enemy, because it was not a big enough attack to be anything but a feint.

General Haking, conforming to the usual practice of blaming others, said that the attack failed solely because the infantry was new to battle. In fact, apart from poor planning, it failed for five reasons:

1. The objective did not exist, being nothing more than abandoned ditches and trenches, all water-filled.
2. The front was too narrow, therefore the Germans could defend it in depth and readily reinforce it.
3. The German artillery had not been knocked out; throughout the battle gunner observers on Fromelles Ridge directed the guns onto the target.
4. The British guns had not destroyed the German machine-gun posts.
5. The British 61st Division was not used intelligently and while the Australian 5th was going forward the 61st was static.

Haking's report was characteristic of the times: 'The Australian infantry attacked in a most gallant manner and gained the enemy's position but they were not sufficiently trained to consolidate the ground gained. The attack, though it has failed, has done both divisions a great deal of good.'

In fact, his attack had crippled the 5th Division and had begun the process of making the AIF critical of British generalship on the Western Front. Australian officers were well aware that Haking's attack was a self-indulgence, that of a general who wanted to make a name for himself by fighting a battle. Since by some perverted logic British generals assessed success by the number of their own casualties, Fromelles did Haking's reputation a lot of good. With 25 per cent casualties he had acquitted himself well.

Brigadier-General H.E. Elliott, who commanded the Australian 15th Brigade during the battle, understood why the attack had failed: 'The whole operation was so incredibly blundered from beginning to end that it is almost incomprehensible how the British Staff, who were responsible for it, could have consisted of trained professional soldiers of considerable reputation and experience, and why, in the outcome of this extraordinary adventure, any of them were retained in active command.'

After the disaster Captain Philip Landon,[4] a captain on the staff of 182nd Infantry Brigade said, 'The weakness of GHQ lay in not seeing that a Corps commander, left to himself, would also be tempted to win glory for his Corps by a spectacular success, and would be prodigal in using the divisions that passed through his hands for this purpose.'

Haig's letters and diary entries contain many references to his faith in Divine help. God was giving him strength, support and guidance. But by the middle of July he was no longer mentioning God. Some writers believe that as the decisive result he wanted was no longer attainable there was no need to call on God. My feeling is that he felt, perhaps in his deep subconscious, that God had let him down. Possibly he felt that he had asked God for too much.

To achieve what God had not, Haig turned instead to the Australians. He wanted them to capture Poziéres village and ridge, for without them he could not encircle the powerful German fortress-like positions at Thiepval which dominated the Ancre river valley. The AIF divisions were part of the British Reserve Army, whose GOC was General Sir Hubert Gough. At the age of forty-six, Gough was the youngest of the Army commanders and his arrogance made him universally disliked. Educated at Eton and Sandhurst, he had a mostly cavalry background and had commanded the 16th Lancers and the 3rd Cavalry Brigade. He was regarded as a tough GOC and he certainly acted tough, for he wanted battle progress at any price.

Field Marshals Sir John French,
Earl Kitchener and Sir Douglas
Haig; from World War I
postcards

Mesopotamia. Above: The
Strand Basra. Below:
Inspection of India's troops.
Inset: Major-General Charles
Townshend

Gallipoli. Above: Heavy casualties moved by barge. Below: The ridges behind the Anzac sector which the troops were expected to climb, under fire, and capture. Inset: General Sir Ian Hamilton relaxing on board ship

Gallipoli. Major-General Sir Aylmer
Hunter-Weston, commander of VIII Army
Corps outside his dugout. Inset: *Mother,
Mother*. A painting of the Somme by
Alfred Priest

General Sir Henry Seymour
Rawlinson, commander of the
Fourth Army. General Sir Henry
Wilson, Britain's Military
Representative on the Allied
War Canal. 'The King at the
Front', from a World War I
postcard.

Passschendaele. Above: Part of the quagmire at
Passchendaele. Below: A track between
Broodseinde and Passchendaele. Inset: General
Sir Hubert de la Poer Gough, commander of the
Fifth Army.

Ypres. Above: Digging out the wounded, near Zillebeke, 20 September 1917. Below: Ditched, a British tank of 1918. Inset: General the Hon. Sir Julian Byng, commander of the Third Army

The Somme. Above: Infantry ordered 'over the top' to certain heavy casualties. Below: Death and destruction in the trenches. Inset: Lieut-General Sir Lancelot Kiggell

By 17 July Poziéres had already been unsuccessfully assaulted three times. Now Haig told Gough to 'carry out operations against Poziéres with a view to capturing this important position with as little delay as possible.' Gough sent for Lieut.-General H.E. Walker, GOC AIF 1st Division and said, 'I want you to go into the line and attack Poziéres tomorrow night.'

This was extremely short notice and Walker demurred, but Gough overruled him and on 19 July Walker moved his men from their rear areas to take up a front of 1 mile. The division's objective included the large ruin of Mouquet Farm, which was honeycombed with underground passages.

On the night of 23/24 July the Australians captured most of their objectives and on the 24th and 25th they took the rest of Poziéres. After enduring 3 days of shattering shellfire the division was withdrawn, with the loss of 5,285 officers and men. By now Poziéres was 'nothing but a churned mass of debris with bricks, stones and girders and bodies pounded to nothing. There are not even tree trunks left, not a leaf, not a twig, all is buried and churned up again and again and buried again.'[5]

From 23 July, Haig's control of operations did not go beyond a few maxims and vague observations. He left everything to Gough until 15 September and Gough's creed was speed. Such an aim would have been not merely acceptable but commendable in other conditions, however, in narrow-fronted trench battles it was dangerous.

He now brought in the AIF 2nd Division (Major-General J.G. Legge) and it was at once plunged into terrible fighting. During a 12½-hour bomb fight the Australians threw 15,000 grenades – and had as many thrown at them. The 2nd Division spent 12 days on Poziéres Ridge where they were subjected to repeated heavy shelling and were in action almost continuously. It lost 6,848 officers and men and five of its battalions were almost wiped-out.

The AIF 4th Division was ordered in on the night of 5 August for its share of Gough's bloodbath. During ferocious fighting in the period 7–8 August the 48th Battalion lost 20 officers and 578 men, the 45th lost 5 officers and 340 men, mostly from shellfire. In six successive night attacks the division advanced the British line within striking distance of Mouquet Farm.

Gough watched carefully to judge exactly when one division was wilting and a fresh one was needed. He pushed in the AIF 1st Division, for the second time, to relieve the 4th. It stayed on the ridge until 22 August, losing another 92 officers and 2,558 men, including 850 in a brave attack on Mouquet Farm. The AIF 2nd Division then returned to the ridge and was in almost constant action until the first week of September. In a particularly bitter fight the 13th Brigade captured part of Fabeck Graben.

It was the only success of Gough's vast movement to encircle Thiepval. The three AIF divisions had suffered 23,000 casualties, or one man in three. Charles Bean was angry about the methods 'of applying a battering-ram ten or fifteen times against the same part of the enemy battle front with the intention of penetrating for a mile into the midst of his organised defences.'

Soldiers' letters illustrate Bean's criticisms. A sergeant[6] who saw the survivors of the 1st Division come out of the battle wrote, 'Although we knew it was stiff fighting we had our eyes opened when we saw these men march by. Those who watched them will never forget it as long as they live. They looked like men who had been in hell. Almost without exception each man looked drawn and haggard and so dazed that they appeared to be walking in a dream, and their eyes looked glassy and starey. Quite a few were silly, and these were the only noisy ones in the crowd.'

'We are lousy, stinking, ragged, unshaven, sleepless,' wrote Lieut. J.A. Raws[7] of the 23rd Battalion. 'My tunic is rotten with other men's blood and partly spattered with a comrade's brains. It is horible but why should you people at home not know?'

Shellbursts twice buried Raws with the dead and dying. 'The ground was covered with bodies in all stages of decay and mutilation, and I would, after struggling free from the earth, pick up a body to lift him out with me, and find him a decayed corpse. I pulled a head off – covered with blood. The horror was indescribable. In the dim, misty light of dawn I collected about 50 men and sent them off, mad with terror, on the right track for home.'

'I want to tell you', Raws says in another letter, 'so that it may be on record, that I honestly believe that Goldie [a mate] and many other officers were murdered through the incompetence, callousness and personal vanity of those high in authority. I realise the seriousness of what I say, but I am so bitter, and the facts so palpable, that it must be said.' He was referring to Haig and Gough and their staffs.

NOTES

GHQ, Army, Corps and Divisional reports provide the battle base for this chapter. As always, the detailed accounts by the Australian Official Historian, C.E.W. Bean, provide reliable and detailed evidence of AIF involvement in the battles and campaigns. Bean is generally considered to be the most thorough chronicler of the war from the middle of 1916 to the end of the conflict.

1. George Coppard went to the war in 1914 and served as a machine-gunner until 1917 when he was badly wounded. He wrote about his experiences in *With a Machine-Gun to Cambrai*, published by Imperial War Museum, 1969.
2. Graham Greenwell began the war as an 18-year-old 2nd Lieutenant in the Oxfordshire and Buckinghamshire Light Infantry. He wrote about his experiences in 1972.
3. The Countess Haig published her biography of her husband, *The Man I Knew*, in 1936. Her loyalty, devotion and love for him is evident throughout the book.
4. Captain Landon made this comment to the British Official Historian, Brigadier-General J. Edmonds.
5. Bean, op cit.
6. E.J. Rule of the 14th Battalion, in his book *Jacka's Mob*, Sydney, 1933.
7. Raws, a journalist of Melbourne, was killed by a shellburst at Poziéres on 23 August. His brother was killed at Poziéres on 29 July.

8

HAIG and the H.C.I. FIXATION

'Something to Answer For'

C.E.W. BEAN, AUSTRALIAN OFFICIAL HISTORIAN

In support of Haig, the Press back in England were assuring the anxious populace that they need not worry unduly about the boys across the Channel doing battle with the Huns. A Special Correspondent of the *Morning Post*, writing on 7 August stated, 'As for the bayonet, the German soldier never stands up against it. He calls it "the English terror". He simply drops on his knees, and with cries of "Kamerad! Kamerad!" begs piteously for mercy.'

On the day this nonsense was published the Australians were engaged in a life-and-death struggle at Poziéres and the Germans had inflicted 200,000 casualties on the British armies in 5 weeks.

With the Australians used up, Gough ordered in the Canadians for their share of slaughter. Like the Australians before them, they captured a little ground and suffered more than 20,000 casualties. At Guillemont, High Wood and Ginchy British units attacked again and again. The New Zealand division lost heavily at Longueval. The battle seemed endless.

In August Winston Churchill wrote a memorandum in which he attacked the conduct of the Somme offensive.[1] He said that he:

viewed with the utmost pain, the terrible and disproportionate slaughter of our troops. We have not conquered in a month's fighting as much ground as we were expected to gain in the first two hours. We have not advanced two miles in a direct line at any point. Unless a gap of at least 20 miles can be opened, no large force can be put through. Nor are we making for any point of strategic or political consequence. What are Peronne and Bapaume, even if we are likely to take them? The open country towards which we are struggling by inches is capable of entrenched defence at every step and is utterly devoid of military significance. There is no question of breaking the line, of "letting loose the cavalry" in the open country behind or of inducing a general withdrawal of the German armies in the West. In personnel the results of the operation have been absolutely barren.

Haig's ally in London, Robertson, the CIGS, wrote to Haig, 'The powers-that-be are beginning to get a little uneasy. The casualties are mounting up and they are wondering whether we are likely to get a proper return for them.'

Haig had plausible good news. Pressure on Verdun had been relieved. The world now knew that the Allies could maintain a vigorous defensive. He had driven the enemy's best troops from their positions and had inflicted 'very heavy losses' on them. By keeping up the steady pressure Germany would be completely overthrown.

Then, almost like a PS, he added the bad news that there would need to be another campaign in 1917. He would have broken through in August, he said, but certain officers had not made thorough preparations.

He proposed to make a final attempt to break through the German defences, reach open country and capture Bapaume. To do this he decided to use the new war machines called 'tanks'. Fifty-nine of them had arrived in France, but they were there only for further trials and experiments and for training crews. Haig decided to use them in battle. In a letter to Robertson, he wrote: 'Even if I do not get as many as I hope, I shall use whatever I have got, as I cannot wait any longer for them, and it would be folly not to use any means at my disposal in what is likely to be our crowning effort of the year.'

In fact, it was folly to use them now and Winston Churchill, a sponsor of the tanks idea, was shocked. He opposed the exposure of 'this tremendous secret to the enemy upon such a petty scale and as a mere make-weight to what I was sure could only be an indecisive operation.' Other tank sponsors as well as the inventors and cabinet ministers beseeched Haig not to use the tanks, not yet.

Colonel E.D. Swinton urged the High Command to wait until a great mass of tanks was ready to be launched, together with infantry, in a great combined operation. Haig persisted with his intention to use the available tanks at Flers as soon as possible. Just as he had wasted the New Armies, he was now going to waste the tanks.

Lloyd George visited the Front at this time and with the evidence of his own eyes, he questioned Allied tactics.[2] 'When I ventured to express to Generals Joffre and Haig my doubts as to whether cavalry could ever operate successfully on a front bristling for miles behind the enemy lines with barbed wire and machine guns both generals fell on me. The conversation gave me an idea of the exaltation produced in brave men by battle. They were quite incapable of looking beyond or even through the struggle just in front of them.'

Haig's great day was fixed for 15 September. Only 32 machines reached the assembly area in a fit state to go forward. Contrary to the principles laid down by the tank pioneers, Haig allowed 24 tanks to go into battle in piecemeal actions. Most broke down, became bogged or were knocked out by shellfire. It was a tragic and needless waste. Only 4, at Flers, were effective. They had been tragically and needlessly wasted. Had they been massed in one sector, instead of spread about the battlefield, they may have broken through and led the infantry into Bapaume.

Only 18 of the monstrous tanks were useful in action and though they lumbered slowly they gave the German troops a fearful surprise. On that day the Canadians took Courcellette, the Scots seized Martinpuich and High Wood was finally captured. One tank drove down the battered main street at Flers. However, by afternoon the Germans had sealed off the British breach and

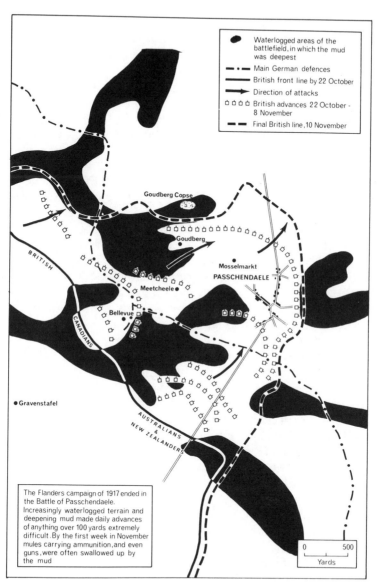

Waterlogged areas of the battlefield, in which the mud was deepest

Main German defences

British front line by 22 October

Direction of attacks

British advances 22 October - 8 November

Final British line, 10 November

Goudberg Copse

Goudberg

Mosselmarkt

PASSCHENDAELE

BRITISH

Meetcheele

CANADIANS

Bellevue

Gravenstafel

AUSTRALIANS & NEW ZEALANDERS

The Flanders campaign of 1917 ended in the Battle of Passchendaele. Increasingly waterlogged terrain and deepening mud made daily advances of anything over 100 yards extremely difficult. By the first week in November mules carrying ammunition, and even guns, were often swallowed up by the mud

0   500
Yards

Passchendaele: the mud

the battlefield was littered with abandoned tank hulks.

The generals were enthusiastic and orders for a thousand tanks were placed, but the tank pioneers and Churchill were depressed. 'This priceless conception', Churchill wrote, 'was revealed to the Germans for the mere petty purpose of taking a few ruined villages.'[3]

On 25 September the push continued but no victory was in sight, as a British officer discerned:[4] 'One can compare our whole offensive to a little boy who sets out to climb a big tree. On failing to reach the first bough he takes out a pocketknife and proceeds to cut it down. That is what we are doing. On the 26th the tree, after three months of cutting, was showing a little weakness through loss of sap.'

Haig's unworried attitude to his own casualties is shown, yet again, in his diary entry of 27 September 1916. His adjutant-general had reported that casualties in 2 days' heavy fighting had been 8,000. 'This is very remarkable,' Haig comments – and he did not mean remarkably high but remarkably low. He thought that so *few* British casualties had to mean that the Germans were not fighting so well or had suffered in morale.

Haig seemed unable to grasp the enormity of his own losses and the lack of real progress, for on 30 September 'Lucky' Haig confided to his diary, 'Luckily, matters are going well with the British Army here.' He based this partly on opinion emanating from French Army HQ that the British Army had nothing to learn from the French. This may have been true but it did not mean that the British Army had nothing whatever to learn.

After visiting the Front in 1916, George Bernard Shaw wrote of Haig: 'He was, I should say, a man of chivalrous and scrupulous character. He made me feel that the war would last thirty years, and that he would carry it on irreproachably until he was superannuated.'

Parts of Haig's life-style showed that he had settled down for a long stay at Montreuil, 60 miles from the trenches. Philip Gibbs, the war correspondent, often saw the Commander-in-Chief at GHQ. 'It was', says Gibbs,[5] 'a place where the pageantry of war still maintained its old and dead tradition. One often saw the

Commander-in-Chief starting for an afternoon ride, a fine figure, nobly mounted, with two ADCs and an escort of Lancers. A pretty sight, with fluttering pennons on their lances and horses groomed to the last hair. It was prettier than the real thing up in the Salient [Ypres] or beyond the Somme, where dead bodies lay on upheaved earth among ruins and slaughtered trees. War at Montreuil was quite a pleasant occupation for elderly generals.'

Everything was simplistic at Army and GHQ level. For instance, any attack that failed with heavy casualties was regarded sympathetically and the leaders were not penalised. But every attack that failed with light casualties was condemned without inquiry and the commander of the day received, at best, a black mark on his record, or was sent home in disgrace.

There was, therefore, strong pressure on senior officers to press their attacks, no matter how obviously hopeless, if only to prove that they had tried to the limit of their men's endurance. A brigadier-general who lost half his men in an attack had obviously done well. The point can easily be proved. For instance, in early September 1916, the 49th Division failed to hold positions along the Ancre River. Haig was angry and bluntly told the divisional commander and his staff that the failure was the result of the troops not really attacking 'because total losses of this division are under a thousand.'

On 2 October rain turned the battlefield into a sea of mud in which any movement was immensely difficult. As the weather became colder the conditions were appalling, and even the march to leave the line, after relief, was an agony. 'On either side of the track exhausted men of the incoming division were lying, slowly drowning in the mud. What else could you do except give them the contents of your flask?'[6]

On 21 October Haig regarded an attack by units of the Reserve Army as 'very successful'. According to figures supplied to him, all objectives had been gained on a front of over 5,000 yards and 300 to 500 yards in depth. About 1,000 prisoners had been taken and British losses were 'under 1,600'. But this was the equivalent of two battalions.

Haig continued fighting into a wet and cold November mainly

because of his ingenuous view that the general who held on the longest would win. Almost every day he questioned his Chief of Intelligence, Brigadier General John Charteris, about German morale. Charteris, a sycophant, dutifully told Haig what he wanted to hear – that enemy morale was falling. In fact, as any battalion intelligence officer in the mud at Flers could have told him, it was rising. Some senior officers at GHQ knew this but they were frightened of giving Haig information which they knew he would not want to accept, so they stayed silent.

On 6 November Haig made an expansive offer to the French. He would continue to 'operate offensively' during the winter, to the utmost extent of his resources and opportunities, 'in order to hold the enemy's forces in our front and to wear them down as much as possible.'

Gough was largely responsible for the futile and costly attacks on the Somme which went on that month, when soldiers could barely drag one foot after another out of the mud. Pigheadedly confident – he did not have to drag his own feet out of the sucking mud – Gough remained a disciple of the offensive at all costs, even with exhausted, sick men. He proposed to send 11 Corps, under Major-General Jacob, into an attack at Grandcourt. Jacob was on the spot and had sound information about conditions and he reported that his judgment was that such an attack was hopeless. Gough forced Jacob to make the attack. It failed and, as usual, was costly.

With Herculean striving, the British troops captured Le Sars village, near an ancient burial mound, the Butte of Warlencourt. On that sector the battle had ended. On 13 November, in heavy fog, infantry were thrown at Beaumont-Hamel and St Pierre Divion on the Ancre River and after 5 days the villages were captured. On 18 November, in the first snowstorms, the Big Push, which Herbert Asquith called 'the long and sombre procession of cruelty and suffering', came to a stop. Asquith had reason to be critical; he had lost a son in the battle. In November and December, the Conservative leaders Bonar Law and Edward Carson joined with Lord Beaverbrook to champion the cause of David Lloyd George who, on 7 December, succeeded Asquith as Prime Minister.

HAIG AND THE H.C.I. FIXATION

As the Battle of the Somme came to its bloody end in the mud, a voice of protest about the waste and lunacy was heard. Robert Graves and Siegfried Sassoon wrote bitter poems. Leslie Coulson should be included here, though he had been killed in October. His last poem challenged the leaders to explain themselves:

> Who made the Law that men should die in meadows?
> Who spake the word that blood should splash in lanes?
> Who gave it forth that gardens should be boneyards?
> Who spread the hills with flesh, and blood and brains?
> Who made the law?
> But who made the Law? The trees shall whisper to him:
> 'See, see the blood – the splashes on our bark'
> Walking the meadows, he shall hear bones crackle
> And fleshless mouths shall gibber in silent lanes at dark.
> Who made the law?

Bertrand Russell the philosopher, and H.W. Massingham the editor, inveighed against the futility but Lord Northcliffe's *War Book* brought some patronising comfort in the midst of gloom:

Our soldiers are individual. They embark on little individual enterprises. The German is not so clever at these devices. He was never taught them before the war, and his whole training from childhood upwards had been to obey, and to obey in numbers. He has not played individual games. Football, which develops individuality, has only been introduced into Germany in comparatively recent times.

Perhaps if the Germans had been better football players they would have been more sporting on the battlefield. As it was, they seemed to be taking the killing all too seriously. But then, according to the *New Statesmen*, the Allies were serious-minded as well. The journal exalted heroism and exulted in self-sacrifice:

Men go voluntarily to their death in a manner that has amazed all who held that the European races had grown decadent and had lost their courage. Obviously thousands of young men are living in the spirit of Achilles. There is nothing in the record of human warfare –

no, not the glory of Marathon or Thermopylae – to surpass this epic of courage and self-sacrifice that is being written all over the face of Europe today.

The official figures for 'self-sacrifice' set the British Empire's total casualties at 419,654, but such exactitude is suspect. Almost certainly they were greater. The French lost 204,000. It is said that 500,000 Germans became casualties, but there is an element of British–French exaggeration in this. The leaders *wanted* to believe that half a million Huns had been accounted for. It is true that General Ludendorff admitted that his army had been 'fought to a standstill and was utterly worn out,' but the Allies were even more worn out.

Haig liked to claim the Somme as a victory. In his despatch of 13 December 1916 he disregarded his original breakthrough plan and claimed that he had wanted a battle of attrition all along. The claim has been proved spurious. Liddell Hart observed,[7] 'Haig failed to break through and because he failed, his defenders have argued that it was never his main purpose. If this were true – and it isn't – the most rational reason for his conduct of the battle disappears.'

In February 1917 the German army withdrew to its new and massively strong defence system the Siegfried Line – or what British history knows as the Hindenberg Line. The Germans gave up 1,000 square miles of French territory but shortened their line by 32 miles. Their new dispositions did not constitute a British victory but, naturally enough, Haig claimed that it did.

The French war historian Marc Ferro considers that Haig and the French leaders behaved with 'criminal stubbornness'. The Somme battle, Ferro says,[8] 'was disastrous in the loss it caused, almost useless from the military viewpoint and merely revealed the vainglory of the generals. Haig's narrow-minded obstinacy was matched by Foch's unflinching confidence.'

Bean says the British part in the battle of the Somme was 'the logical outcome of dull, determined strategy and the devotion of an inexperienced army.'

Far from the German loss being greater, C.E.W. Bean says,[9] the British and Empire armies were being worn down, numerically speaking, more than twice as fast. But the loss cannot be measured merely by numbers. The troops who bore the brunt of the Somme fighting were – to quote Bean – 'the cream of the British population, the new volunteer army. Inspired by lofty altruistic ideals traditional in British upbringing, in high purity of aim and single-minded sacrifice it was probably the finest army that ever went to war. Despite the indignation expressed by one of the higher commanders at the criticism current in England, a general who wears down 180,000 of his enemy by expending 400,000 [of his own] men of this quality has something to answer for.' The figures are Bean's estimate of the comparative losses.

Perhaps the most biting comment on the Battle of the Somme is made by Lovat Fraser:[10] 'Our High Command had not advanced beyond the tactics of the Stone Age. They had not conceived any form of warfare except the blind fighting of masses of docile men against formidable positions month after month.'

Boraston and Dewar, writing in 1922, saw the struggle in a quite different way: 'The battle of the Somme was a great triumph for the genius of British leadership,' they say. Looking back from a perspective of nearly 70 years, one can only wonder how they could make this statement and believe that they were speaking the truth. If they made the statement believing it to be honest how could they have so grossly deluded themselves? Perhaps because of the imperative need to escape from the shocking truth that the battle was a shocking debacle. Perhaps out of loyalty to a man whom they liked and wished to protect.

On 23 December 1916 Haig sent his final despatch on the Somme. In it he made this statement: 'Machine-guns play a great part – almost a decisive part under some conditions – in modern war.' At long last he had discovered what his junior officers and all the rank-and-file – those who had to do the fighting – had known since August 1914, and what Lloyd George had anticipated from the same time. And yet, having uncovered this secret of successful warfare Haig would, in 1917, send tens of thousands of more men to their deaths against German machine-guns in the Ypres Salient and elsewhere.

NOTES

As before, statements by Haig come from his diary, letters or despatches, or from the Official History.

1. Winston Churchill, *The World Crisis*, Butterworth, 1927.
2. David Lloyd George, *War Memoirs*, Odhams, 1938.
3. Churchill, op cit.
4. Lieut. Christian Creswell Carver, Royal Field Artillery, in a letter home. He was killed on 23 July 1917.
5. Basil Liddell Hart, *Realities of War*, Heinemann, 1920.
6. A. Hanbury-Sparrow, *The Land-Locked Lake*, Barker, 1932.
7. Basil Liddell Hart, op cit.
8. Marc Ferro, *The Great War 1914–1918*, Editions Gallimard, 1969.
9. C.E.W. Bean, op cit.
10. Quoted by P.A. Thompson in his *Lions Led by Donkeys*, Werner Laurie, 1927.

CARNAGE at PASSCHENDAELE

'This Senseless and Bloody Struggle'

ARTHUR BEHRAND, IN ACTION AT YPRES

King George V's 1917 New Year's gift to 'Lucky' Haig was promotion to the rank of Field Marshal.

A former Secretary of State for War, Lord Haldane, certainly approved for he wrote to Haig on 4 January:

> You are almost the only military leader we possess with the power to think, which the enemy possess in a highly developed form. The necessity of a highly trained mind, and of the intellectual equipment which it carries, is at last recognised among our people. In things other than military they have, alas, most things still to learn, but in the science and art of war a trying experience has dictated the necessity of a gift such as yours won by the hard toil of the spirit.

Some people might not have considered that the conduct of the Somme battle warranted promotion to the pinnacle of British Army rank.

The British Army owed much to Lord Haldane and it was largely due to him that in 1914 Britain had its highly-trained Expeditionary Force of 160,000 men. Haig had been Haldane's assistant before the war.

Lord Haldane had a cousin, Lieut.-General Sir Aylmer Haldane, serving under Haig. General Haldane had much the same views as Haig and Rawlinson on infantry tactics. As early as 1909 he had advocated a thick attacking body of infantry when storming trenches held by an enemy armed with machine-guns. Infantry could not win battles merely by avoiding loss, Haldane had said at a conference. He was a great advocate of leaders getting their men to cheer as loudly as possible in an attack, 'so as to effect, by vibration, the enemy's nerves.' Certainly he said this before he knew that his next enemy would be the Germans, who were not noted for breaking under the vibration caused by cheers. Still, these and others of Haldane's observations indicate that his 'intellectual equipment' was on a par with that of his Commander-in-Chief.

The five Army commanders paid Haig a practical compliment on his promotion. They chipped in to buy him the jewelled baton which went with his new rank.

In France and Belgium most soldiers did not hear about the great promotion but it would not have excited them. It is unlikely to have elicited more than a grunt of acknowledgement. The men's attention and energies were almost entirely taken up by coping with the elements during the winter of 1916–17. It was particularly bitter and in the earlier part any man unwary enough to step off a defined track quickly sank to his armpits in mud. It would take five or six men to pull him out. An Australian officer had his back broken by the strenuous efforts made to free him from the mud.

When the weather froze, so did the mud – and so did the soldiers. Tired, bitterly cold, lice-ridden and often hungry they endured their privations with a kind of animal resignation and consoled themselves with the reflection that, amazingly, they were still alive and that the war was relatively quiet.

Changes were taking place which the troops only vaguely heard about. In the French army Marshal Joffre, as ardent an attritionist as Haig, was replaced with General Robert Nivelle, who had been promoted over the heads of Foch and Petain. Nivelle extravagantly promised tactics which would drive through the German lines in massive strength and end the war at a stroke.

In Germany, von Falkenhayn, who had inflicted tremendous

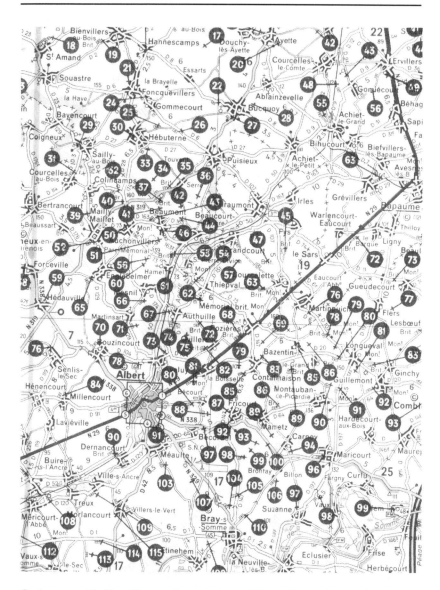

Commonwealth War Graves Commission military cemeteries on the Somme battlefield. Each dot marks a cemetery

casualties on the French at Verdun but who had nevertheless failed to capture the place, was replaced in August 1916 by Field Marshal Paul von Hindenburg and General Erich Ludendorff. This formidable partnership had been successful against the Russians in the Eastern Front campaigns. Ludendorff was the brains of the combination and *de facto* commander of the army in the field. The older Hindenburg, a national and venerated figure, was the 'political' head of the army.

In Britain, Lloyd George's rise to power as Prime Minister seemed likely to bring about radical changes in the military leadership. He distrusted the generals and their tactics and was profoundly apprehensive of further losses on the scale of the Somme slaughter. Having found Kitchener and Haig unable to see the obvious threat of the machine-gun in German hands and its promise in British hands, he feared that the generals would never be able to use new ideas and new equipment.

Lloyd George knew that it would be difficult to remove Haig especially now that he was a Field Marshal. The Haig coterie had powerful friends, of whom the King was the most influential. By the beginning of 1917 the professional military directorates considered themselves not only free from interference by civilian agencies but above the nation itself. Captain Peter Wright[1] expresses this attitude cogently, 'This great deceit at last emancipates all General Staffs from all control. They no longer live for the nation; the nation lives, or rather dies, for them. What matters to these semi-sovereign corporations is whether dear old Willie or poor old Harry is going to be at their head. Two branches of a staff can get more hostile to each other than to the enemy.'

An example of this military domination of politicians occurred in March 1917 when the Ribot administration, which had succeeded the Briand government in France, proposed that all offensive operations should be deferred until American assistance became available. Haig and Robertson, Petain and Nivelle, thought otherwise. 'We are all of the opinion', wrote Robertson in an official memorandum, 'that our object can be obtained by relentlessly attacking with limited objectives, while making the fullest use of our artillery. By this means we hope to gain our ends with the minimum loss possible.'

Actually, a limited offensive was not what Haig cherished. Ever since he had become C-in-C, he had set his heart on a decisive battle in Flanders and he was so obsessed by this objective that he believed that he could beat the Germans single-handed, and before the Americans came in.

In 1916 and 1917 the size of the forces under his command intrigued Haig and, being ambitious, he was driven to use this great human weapon. The value of economy of force appears not to have occurred to him. The very bulk of the British army was too great for anything but 'big push' tactics. According to Barrie Pitt,[2] 'Haig lacked the intellectual power – or genius – to handle so mighty a weapon as his army with any degree of subtlety.'

The much vaunted Nivelle plan, which called for a joint British and French operation, began on 9 April on the British sector with the Battle of Arras. This offensive, on a 30-mile front, involved the 3rd Army, under General Sir Edmund Allenby, and 5th Army under Gough. It got off to a good start with a brilliant victory by the Canadian Corps in capturing Vimy Ridge. A strategic height, it overlooked an immense area of German-held territory.

The victory at Vimy was the result of intelligent planning by the Canadian commander, Lieut.-General A.W. Currie and his staff, and courageous fighting by the Canadian soldiers. It was one of the most striking successes of the war, but it cost 11,000 Canadian casualties in 5 days.

Allenby's 3rd Army units covered 5 miles, in places, on the first day. Allenby eagerly anticipated a genuine breakthrough but then spoiled his chances by repeating old mistakes. He divided his 40 tanks into small groups and used them on the wrong ground. Some were quickly bogged, others failed the infantry because of poor briefing.

On the adjoining sector, Gough proposed to attack the Hindenburg Line with the Australian 4th Division, recognised as one of the finest infantry formations on the Western Front. Gough planned to put in the division without an artillery barrage and hoped that a few tanks he had laid his hands on would break through the enemy barbed wire.

General Sir William Birdwood, GOC 1 Anzac Corps, and his brilliant Chief-of-Staff, Major-General Cyril Brudenell White, saw many flaws in the plan and questioned it. Typically, Gough overrode them as over other pleas. Without a protective or preliminary barrage, failed by the tanks, the Australians attacked against uncut wire. Incredibly, they broke the Hindenburg Line, something previously considered impossible. But they were left without support. At first the artillery did not fire because of misleading reports, then it fired on its own infantry and finally German machine-gunners cut off the Australian infantry in the trenches which they had captured. The seven battalions and support units involved suffered 3,000 casualties.

Gough sent a message to the 4th Division that he was 'satisfied that the effect upon the whole situation by the Anzac attack had been of great assistance.' The message was justified in terms of morale building but every officer of the 4th Australian Division knew that it had been used with almost maniacal rashness.

His general plan was full of blunders so great that the ordinary soldiers were aware of them. Birdwood decided to face out the situation by confronting the survivors of the AIF 4th Brigade in person. In company with the brigade commander – C.H. Brand – he saw the men in their camp and both officers, 'with tears in their eyes',[3] told the troops about their unsuccessful attempts to have the plans changed. The Australians heard all this in grim silence and then slouched away. They knew Gough's reputation and could believe what Birdwood said.

It is possible that Haig was unaware of Gough's tactical plan, even after Birdwood and White had questioned it. Haig must, however, bear the responsibility for the cover up. No inquiry was called into the Bullecourt disaster. Birdwood and White and other Australian senior officers knew the true story but could not bring it to his attention because of his style of command. Haig and his staff remained ignorant of the conduct of an important operation for which they were responsible. Dewar and Boraston,[4] who went to great lengths to avoid criticisms of any British general, could not later defend Gough over First Bullecourt: 'The scheme of the attack perhaps asked too much both of men and machines at this stage of their training and development,' they say. Until the end of the war British instructors used First Bullecourt as an example of how an attack should not be undertaken.

At Bullecourt, Bean[5] says, Gough's judgment 'showed itself to be the plaything of an almost childish impetuosity.'

Meanwhile, Allenby was also making mistakes of childish impetuosity. Despite every indication to the contrary, he acted on the assumption of a breakthrough and issued a General Order: 'The Army Commander wishes all troops to understand that the 3rd Army is now pursuing a defeated enemy and that risks must be freely taken.' He set an example by ordering in his cavalry near Monchy-le-Preux. Yet another cavalry general in high command, 'The Bull' still nursed delusions about what a cavalry charge could do in modern war.

British infantry watched spellbound as line upon line of mounted men, with lances and sabres, rode quickly down the hillsides. 'It may have been a fine sight,' one of them reported, 'but it was a wicked waste of men and horses for the enemy immediately opened on them a hurricane of every kind of missile. The cavalry advanced through us at a canter but they came back at a gallop.'

Many of the horses were riderless and some were so badly wounded that the shocked infantrymen shot them. The Germans could hardly believe their luck at being presented with such a target and Allenby's cavalry sweep was a disaster. He should have known that it would fail. His decision to keep attacking brought written protests from three of his more rational generals on 14 April. In the face of such opposition Haig had to call a halt.

Fighting was resumed on the Scarpe River and around Bullecourt, where the Australians were involved in a second battle, 3–26 May. By 13 May the gap which they had made in the Hindenburg Line became 2 miles wide. On 15 May, after an intense 18-hour bombardment, the Germans launched élite regiments against the Australians, but within minutes the attack disintegrated and few Germans survived. The winning of the 'impossible' position and the holding of it against seven major counter-attacks was one of the most remarkable achievements of the war, but it cost the 32 Australian battalions involved 7,000 casualties.

The Battle of Arras left 30,000 of Haig's soldiers dead and 128,000 wounded. The French loss was about the same. Nivelle was discredited and removed. Haig survived because he had made no sweeping promises of a grand breakthrough. Haig had never taken Nivelle's plan seriously and he was relieved to be able to turn back to his own plan, an offensive on the north of the Western Front aimed at reaching the Belgian coast. In the Ypres Salient he proposed to strike north-east towards Passchendaele village and the ridge on which it lay. Having smashed the German lines, the cavalry would at last fan out, sweep all before it and capture Ostend and Zeebrugge, the German U-boat bases. In addition, Haig planned to hold down massive German reserves until the new French commander, Petain, had hammered the demoralised and mutinous French army back into shape.

Lloyd George was convinced that the attack in Flanders had not the remotest chance of success. Maurice Hankey,[6] as secretary to the War Council, noted that Lloyd George foresaw the results with 'uncanny prescience'. All his colleagues had grave doubts about the offensive's prospects, though they may have been less sure about the prospects of the plan to send heavy guns to Italy for a campaign against the Austrians. Haig and Robertson had strongly criticised this scheme. Admiral Jellicoe had backed the Flanders plan and was gloomy about what might happen in the English Channel if the Flemish coast was not cleared of Germans. Hankey believed that Lloyd George had the better arguments and that if the question could be decided exclusively on its merits, then the Italian plan should be tried.

Hankey thought that the decision to strike in Flanders was inevitable. The decision to allow Haig to undertake the Flanders offensive was taken by Lloyd George and most of his colleagues with reluctance and misgivings. No one believed that a strategical result could be achieved and all shrank from the terrible losses which they knew it must involve. But as Hankey observed, 'the consensus of naval and military opinion was so overwhelming that the War Cabinet could not take the responsibility of rejecting the advice thrust upon them with so much cogency.'

General Sir Herbert ('Plum') Plumer, who had commanded on the Ypres Salient for 2 years, was the obvious choice to plan and make the assault. Importantly, he was an infantryman with an understanding of what foot soldiers might reasonably be asked to do. With typical care, Plumer studied Haig's requirements and said that they were too ambitious. Disappointed in Plumer, Haig then considered Rawlinson for the job. After his mauling on the Somme, Rawlinson agreed with Plumer.

Haig turned to the thrusting, dynamic Gough, whose sublime confidence had in no way been damaged by the disaster caused by his bungling at Bullecourt. 'We can beat the Germans where and when we like', he had said a few weeks before his appointment. Apparently, nobody asked him why he had not already done so. Gough had nothing like Plumer's familiarity with the Ypres ground and the limits it placed on offensive action, a simple fact which Haig knew when he appointed him on 13 May to fight the Third Ypres.

Plumer had been preparing an attack to destroy a wedge which the Germans had driven into the British Salient on Messines Ridge, south of Ypres. He continued with this while Gough and his Fifth Army HQ planned the Third Battle of Ypres, or Passchendaele as it became popularly known.

Aged sixty, white-haired and with a bushy white moustache and receding chin, Plumer looked more like a senior civil servant cast as a general in a play. But he really was every inch a general, with an unusual degree of consideration for his troops. Battalion commanders liked to find themselves under the command of this thorough and cautious man.

Lieut. Arthur Behrand[7] says that it was common knowledge that the Second Army, under Plumer, looked after its troops better than any of the other armies. 'Hence Plumer, a small man with pink cheeks, was rated as good general. He remains in my mind's eye as a father, even a grandfather figure.'

Plumer planned to blow the enemy off Messines ridge with

shells and mines. Since 1915 British, Australian and Canadian miners had been digging tunnels through the clay and under the enemy positions. Some tunnels were more than 3,000 feet in length. In the labyrinths which developed in this sector, British and German miners fought hand-to-hand, often in pitch blackness, or tried to kill each other by blowing the enemy tunnels and entombing the miners.

By the end of June 1917, 21 great mines, with a total weight of 1 million lbs., were in place under the Germans trenches along a 3-mile line. The largest consisted of nearly 96,000lb. of ammonal. Meanwhile, Plumer assembled 2,266 guns, including 756 heavy weapons, which opened a 16-day bombardment on an 8-mile front. They fired 3,500,000 shells.

Shortly before 3 a.m. on 7 June the British guns fell silent. The silence alarmed the Germans who at once sent up flares to illuminate the battlefield. At 3.10 a.m. 19 of the mines were blown. The effect was devastating and the ground heaved as if in the throes of an earthquake. The roar was heard in London and, according to some reports, in Dublin, 500 miles away.

Into the smoke and ruin stormed nine divsions of British, Australian, New Zealand and Irish troops. In many places they were unopposed. The mine explosions had obliterated 10,000 Germans and many of the survivors were helplessly shocked and useless. By 9 a.m. the ridge was in British hands.

The ever resilient Germans rallied, reinforcements were rushed in and east of the ridge a bloody battle raged for 7 days. The German commander in Flanders, Crown Prince Rupprecht of Bavaria, ordered General von Armin's Fourth Army to fall back and then counter-attack. This manoeuvre limited the British advance. Messines was a dramatic success by trench warfare standards but in the end the manpower loss went in the Germans' favour; they suffered 100,000 casualties to the British 150,000. Yet again it had been shown that the attackers suffered greater losses than the defenders, even after the Germans' great initial loss on the first day of the Battle of Messines.

Lady Haig, in her book about her husband, *The Man I Knew*, devoted two pages to the Messines offensive, but did not mention that the planning and the credit belonged to Plumer; she did not even mention Plumer's name. Every word she wrote implied that the operation was wholly her husband's doing.

Haig saw Messines merely as a prelude to the much greater battle for the Passchendaele Ridge – but the War Cabinet was hesitant about permitting this. At least, they said, the operation should be postponed until Petain could assist with it. One factor in support of the Haig plan was British alarm about shipping losses due to the U-boat menace. If the loss were not reduced it might be difficult for the British to wage war into 1918. Haig travelled to London to put his case and, for a man considered to be inarticulate, he was persuasive. The German army, he told the Prime Minister and his colleagues, was near 'breaking point' and severe British losses could be avoided. Robertson backed Haig and on 20 July the Cabinet consented. On 31 July Haig embarked on the Third Ypres. It was to exceed in horror anything he had yet attempted.

The rain which was now falling posed a problem. The 4½-mile wide battlefield of low-lying ground was prevented from becoming a swamp by an intricate system of dykes and culverts. Shellfire would destroy the system but without shellfire the German defenders would be that much stronger to resist the British assault.

The senior Tank Corps staff officer, Colonel J.F.C. Fuller,[8] was alarmed by the prospect of heavy shelling. 'As we could make no headway against Gough's determination to sink his army in a bottomless bog, we took up the question with GHQ. We pointed out that much of the ground we were to attack over had been reclaimed from the sea, and that bombardment would convert it into a bog. We might just as well have appealed to a brick wall.'

Two weeks' of shelling did indeed make the area into a bog. Half the tanks were lost in the quagmire in the first battle and the rest were of little use. The tremendous British artillery barrage was supposed to wipe out many German batteries, but the four Corps which made the attack dragged themselves forward under a deluge of enemy shells. In one sector explosions destroyed

British telephone communications so thoroughly that Corps and Divisional HQs were cut off from Army HQ for 5 hours.

Under Ludendorff's direct orders, German tactics had changed and were even more effective than ever before. Guns were well protected by emplacements, as were machine-guns, whose crews fired them from within blockhouses or pillboxes, or from on top of these shellproof structures once the British guns had lifted off them.

In front, the German infantry had been much thinned out. Realising that trenches were impossible to maintain in the boggy ground and under British gunfire, the German command defended its forward positions with small groups of men in fortified posts. The great mass of infantry were kept in the rear to act as tactical reserves for counter-attacks. They were launched once the British troops had captured a defensive line. Before they could consolidate, the counter-attack swept forward. This proved to be a very successful tactic.

At the end of the first day, Gough's troops on the right were only 500 yards further forward; on the left they had amazingly moved forward 2 miles, but this was only half the planned distance.

In dreadful conditions, Gough made two more attacks during August. When they failed, with great loss of life, he reported to Haig that tactical success was unlikely or could only be achieved at too high a price.

That month Colonel C.D. Baker-Carr of the Tank Corps delivered a lecture in which he maintained that to continue fighting in the third battle of Ypres was pointless. Brigadier-General John Davidson, Haig's Director of Operations, severely reprimanded him. Baker-Carr explained that the appalling conditions made further fighting just about impossible. Davidson replied that things could not be as bad as Baker-Carr said.

Baker-Carr asked, 'Have you ever been there yourself?'

'No.'

'Has anyone from Operations been there?'

'No,' Davidson admitted.

That very month Rawlinson wrote an appreciation – the army

term – about British command on the Western Front. Considering that his future was largely in Haig's hands, Rawlinson was surprisingly candid, for he said that the High Command had never attempted to conduct a wearing-down battle with planned, logical methods but had relied too much on its belief that a breakdown of the German army's morale was within sight:

> We have never yet set ourselves deliberately to carry out a battle of attrition on absolutely definite lines, with successive objectives well within covering range of the artillery and well within the physical capacity of the infantry. We have never issued hard and fast orders that these objectives were not to be exceeded, however easily they may be gained. We have never set ourselves to work to deliver a succession of carefully worked out hammer blows on the enemy at short intervals with the object of definitely beating him to his knees so that there is no question that his morale is finally broken. Then, and not till then, shall we be able to take liberties. When that stage is reached, moreover, we shall know it instinctively. It will not be a matter of conjecture built up on the reports of prisoners and deserters. It will be an established fact known to every man in our own as well as in the enemy's ranks.

It is unlikely that Haig heard of Baker-Carr's objections for Davidson and Charteris, Haig's Chief of Intelligence, kept such unwelcome opinions from him. But he certainly knew of Gough's assessment of failure and of Rawlinson's advice, which he ignored.

The acutely intelligent Hankey, who was aware of virtually everything that was happening in the upper echelons of power, believes that Lloyd George and the War Cabinet should have intervened as soon as it became clear that the Flanders offensive was making no progess. In Hankey's view, this moment arrived on 15 August.

The fighting had overtaxed and discouraged the British troops but their stubborn Commander-in-Chief did not realise this, even though it was obvious to everyone in touch with the reality of the battlefield. The war correspondent Philip Gibbs knew it. It was obvious to the Germans most of all. From their positions they saw the British infantry stagger through the mud to attack them. Examination of statements by German prisoners showed that Haig's attacks, aimed at destruction of German morale, were in fact wearing down the morale of the British. That Gough, a man accustomed to denial of reality, advised an end to the campaign was a measure of the desperate nature of the situation.

Yet, on 21 August, Haig reported to the War Cabinet that he was 'most satisfied'. He could say this despite having suffered 68,000 casualties in Flanders. Lloyd George, not as satisfied as Haig, took steps to find out about Haig's future intentions and summoned him from France. He did his utmost to induce Haig to change his plans for the capture of the high ground at Passchendaele but Haig and Robertson, with others, obstructed the Prime Minister and kept their fatal optimism.

Having put the Prime Minister in his place, and being disappointed in Gough, Haig transferred control of the Salient operations to Plumer, who now did not have the excuse that he was busy with the Messines operation. Nevertheless, being a steady-push general rather than a breakthrough type, Plumer asked for 3 weeks while he reorganised the large force now under his control. His Second Army would work with Gough's Fifth Army. The Germans on the higher ground contented themselves with artillery fire and with it caused 16,000 British and Empire casualties during the pause. Their shooting was accurate because from their greater height they could observe nearly every movement on the watery, devastated terrain below them.

In September, Plumer fought a series of set-piece battles, all built around the proven battle prowess of the Australians and New Zealanders and a few crack British divisions. In fighting planned by their own Corps HQ, always itself under the guiding hand of Brudenell White, the Anzacs were victorious in the Battles of Menin Road and Polygon Wood.

After Polygon Wood an Australian soldier, Sapper L.J. McKay[9] wrote, 'Mates I have played with last night and joked with are now lying cold. My God it was terrible. Just slaughter. The 5th Div were almost annihilated. We certainly gained our objectives but what a cost.' The AIF lost 17,000 men in this fighting and advanced 4,200 yards.

Even the German use of mustard gas failed either to stop the

Anzacs' advance or to upset Plumer's methodical tactics. It was a superb performance by tired men fighting in heartbreaking conditions.

Between 29 September and 2 October adjustments were made to the front. The Germans, despite their mauling, were still causing casualties. On 30 September one of the dead was Lieut.-Colonel Humphrey Scott, CO of the Australian 56th Battalion. Aged only twenty-five and considered one of the finest battalion commanders of the AIF, Scott volunteered to stay behind, when his men were relieved, to show his British successor the Polygon Wood front. He was shot dead while doing so.

On that day General Rawlinson wrote in his diary: 'Lawford dined. In very good form. His Division 11,000 casualties since July 31st.' Presumably Rawlinson did not intend his note to be an approbation of Major-General S.T. Lawford's losses but the style of the diary entry does indicate something of the senior generals' offhand attitude to casualties.

Plumer told Haig that the men had little more to give and that the offensive should be called off. Even the bloody-minded Gough agreed with him. There was now no chance that the Belgian ports – the ultimate objective – could be reached before winter. In any case, the projected amphibious operation in support of Haig's offensive had already been called off. The two Army commanders made their submissions on 7 October.

Haig replied, 'We ought to have only one thought now in our minds, namely, to attack.'

He was proposing to push his men through a slimy, corpse-filled swamp so dreadful that infantry units took 5 hours to cover 1 mile, even without having to fight. Supplies and ammunition could only be taken forward by donkeys or men, who collapsed under the effort. Up to a dozen bearers were needed to get one stretcher case to the rear.

When a man was left helpless by a wound he marked his position by sticking his rifle in the mud, bayonet down, and hoped desperately for rescue. In most cases help could not reach these men before a German bullet or shell finished them off. Often a wounded man was indistinguishable from the mud – unless he moved. Many drowned in the mud.

Following the 'one thought in his mind', Haig attacked. Between 12–14 October the Australians and New Zealanders captured Broodseinde, part of the Passchendaele Ridge, after incredible exertion and valor. With heavy rain making conditions ever worse, still Haig pressed on. His reasoning was that control of the entire ridge would give him a more easily defended line for the winter. Also, no doubt, he wanted to give his troops the advantage of getting out of the morass for winter.

Winston Churchill,[10] whom Lloyd George had appointed Minister of Munitions in July, had a more realistic idea than Haig about how the war should – and should not – be conducted. During 1916, as a lieut.-colonel, he had been CO of the 6th Royal Fusiliers on the Western Front, so he knew something of the war at the front. In October 1917, as the Australians and New Zealanders were falling in thousands on the slimy slopes of Broodseinde, Churchill wrote that the available strength should not be wasted in 'bloody and indecisive siege operations'. This was his perception of Haig's methods: 'The power of the defensive has produced a deadlock, and the British army is destined to be a holding force throughout 1918 until the Americans can become a decisive factor.'

Here was a concise and accurate assessment of the British predicament and an equally concise solution to it: Sit tight and wait for the Americans. But Haig had no intention of sharing the 'glory' of victory with the untried Americans.

Arthur Behrand, in action with the artillery in the Ypres Salient, would have agreed with Churchill's description of the British operations as 'bloody and indecisive'. Behrand was struck by the immense effort needed to capture a very small objective. He writes:

> If it be true that the seizure of Passchendaele – for to such microscopic proportions had the grandiose objectives of the Third battle of Ypres now been whittled down – was planned mainly for the purpose of saving France and her armies from disintegration, and if Haig's unawareness of the conditions in which his troops were fighting was equally true, I can only say it was a pity he was

not beside me at Menin Gate. For had he witnessed with his own eyes the decimation of so many of his Divisions, he would surely have called a halt to this senseless and bloody struggle for the prize of a few more thousand square feet of mud.

Casualties by their tens of thousands were brought back from the fighting through Ypres' Menin Gate, to relative safety behind the old walls, and were there treated before being sent to the rear.

A comment, in a letter from Lord Esher,[11] brings out the strange and terrible contrast between the sufferings of the soldiers in the front line and the unpleasing squabbles among the highly placed staff officers. Esher had been in the Crillon Hotel, Paris, much used as a meeting place by British senior officers and politicians. On 5 November 1917 he writes, 'There were such crowds of people at the Crillon yesterday. All Paris in the tea-room. L.G. [Lloyd George] came down there and walked about among the people. The soldiers were gathered in groups, representing different "hates". Robertson's lot. Henry Wilson's lot. D.H.'s [Douglas Haig] lot. It was comic. Like the *Chocolate Soldier*, and one expected a chorus, "Thank the Lord the war is over". But it is not – alas.'

The war was far from over but Third Ypres had nearly spent itself, if only because there were not enough fit British and Empire units to keep it going. Also, the infantry was supported by far fewer guns. GHQ and Army HQs apparently did not understand that with heavy use ordnance becomes worn and needs repair. Wear became serious as the guns belched forth thousands of rounds each. It was obvious to the infantry who had to follow the barrages that fewer guns were supporting them but not to those who planned the battle's phases. They simply read their Orders of Battle and noted that the infantry was backed by an adequate number of artillery *units*, without inquiring how many effective guns the units possessed.

An incident related by Edmonds, the official historian,[12] is particularly revealing. At GHQ in October 1917 Colonel A.W. Rawlins, an artillery adviser, told Haig that if his Passchendaele offensive continued no artillery would be available for a 1918 spring offensive. If the guns were not blown out they would be worn out. Turning white with anger, Haig exclaimed, 'Colonel Rawlins, leave the room!' Edmonds, a gunner and engineer, agreed with Rawlins and said so. Haig snapped, 'You go, too!' The episode was reminiscent of Sir John French having told Smith-Dorrien to be silent and do what he was told.

In a final effort – which, with hindsight, seems almost frenzied – Haig threw the Canadians at Passchendaele. Two brigades captured the enemy positions amid the rubble and then, exhausted, collapsed into it. The battle was over.

Since 31 July the British and Empire troops had advanced 5 miles at a cost of at least 250,000 casualties, though some authorities say 300,000. Certainly 100,000 of them occurred after Haig's insistence on continuing the fighting into October. German losses *over the whole* of the Western Front for the same period were about 175,000.

The Germans still held strong lines and their morale was good. After all, they had lived in better conditions than the British throughout the entire battle. Haig claimed that the British offensive had given the French army the peaceful time it needed to recover its strength but it is unlikely that the Germans had contemplated attacking the French lines in any significant way. Haig would have been better advised to show more solicitude for his own men than the French, who expressed little gratitude for the British sacrifice.

Many critics, then and now, considered that however justified Haig may have been in launching the attack in July his decision to keep pushing in October was folly and that his failure to learn from the tragedy of the Somme was inexcusable.

As I see it, to hold on to the quagmire of the Ypres Salient was military lunacy. It was the strategic equivalent of a self-inflicted wound, a court-martial offence.

C.E.W. Bean says,[13] 'Probably a fair judgment of Haig's leadership in the whole battle is – that his determination and loyalty to the general cause ensured the bridging of the most dangerous gap in the effort of the Entente; that he wore down his enemy, though not as quickly as he believed or intended; and that his thrust might, with favourable weather, have attained strategic success. But that the immense cost at which those results were secured could have been much diminished if GHQ had been more closely in touch with the conditions of the battlefield, and Haig's methods more consistently adapted to them.'

Liddell Hart[14] writes of the Third Ypres, 'It would seem that none of the army commanders ventured to press contrary views with the strength that the facts demanded. One of the lessons of the war exemplified at Passchendaele is certainly the need of allowing more latitude in the military system for intellectual honesty and moral courage.'

Passchendaele (Third Ypres) has been called 'the tragic victory'. By the crude yardstick that the British advanced and the Germans retreated, it was technically victory but even this qualified label goes too far. It was not a victory at all – because no benefits derived from it. The Germans could afford to give ground; they had plenty more French and Belgian territory. The Allies could not use the newly won ridge from which to launch a further offensive in an attempt to reach the Belgian coast. German military morale was higher than that of the British.

In his long despatch at the end of the battle – and the end of operations for 1917 – Field-Marshal Haig adopted a characteristically 'what-might-have-been' approach. The despatch was actually prepared by his secretary, Lieut.-Colonel J.H. Boraston. A few sentences illustrate the tenor of the whole document. 'What was actually accomplished under such adverse conditions is the most conclusive proof that, given a normally fine August, the capture of the whole ridge, with the space of a few weeks, was well within the power of the men who achieved so much. . . . The full fruits of each success were not always obtained. Time after time the practically beaten enemy was enabled to reorganise and relieve his men and to bring up reinforcements behind the sea of mud which constituted his main protection.'

With some justice, the last word on Passchendaele might be left to one of the common soldiers who fought there. Rifleman Archie Groom,[15] of the Rifle Brigade, served on the Western

Front continuously for 20 months until he was gassed in May 1918. He says of Paschendaele, 'It is no use trying to whitewash Haig and the General Staff. This is usually done by armchair tacticians who make judgments as if they were playing with toy soldiers, not human beings. After the first few days abortive attempts at a breakthrough nothing of value could be achieved. It became another bloody battle of attrition where so many wounded died lingering deaths in the mud. Third Ypres was a military crime. Haig's diary and the official accounts are monuments of understatement. He appeared to have no idea of front line conditions.'

In using the phrase 'practically beaten enemy' Haig tacitly concedes his own defeat – though this is unintentional. By describing the 'sea of mud' as the Germans' main protection – which was true – he in effect draws attention to his own clumsy tactics, for British barrages had created that protective mud.

'We have every reason to be satisfied with the results which have been achieved by the past years' fighting,' Haig said in his summary.

Such smug complacency at GHQ in Montreuil did not communicate itself to the soldiers in the trenches and miserable billets who had survived the slaughters of 1917. At least General Kiggell, Haig's Chief of General Staff, was not now so complacent. At the end of the Passchendaele fighting, 'Kigg' made his first journey to within a few miles of the front, close enough to find his polished boots sinking into the mud. 'My God,' he said, 'did we really send men to fight in this!' Some reports say that he wept.

It was too late for tears.

NOTES

1. Captain Peter Wright, *At the Surpeme War Council*, New York, 1921.
2. Barrie Pitt has written at length on World War I. This extract is from *The Final Act*, Cassell, 1962.
3. An extract from the diary of Lieut. E.J. Rule of 14th Battalion AIF. Rule's

book, *Jacka's Mob*, Sydney, 1933, is an interesting account of the war as seen by a soldier in the thick of the fighting.

4. George A.B. Dewar and Lieut.-Colonel J.H. Boraston, apologists of the high command, wrote *Sir Douglas Haig's Command*, published in 1922. Boraston also edited *Sir Douglas Haig's Despatches*.

5. C.E.W. Bean, the Australian Official Correspondent and Official Historian. Mentioned in other Chapter notes.

6. Maurice Hankey, later Lord Hankey, was in a unique position to observe the conflict of personalities among the British political and military leaders. His two volumes of *The Supreme Command 1914–1918*, Allen & Unwin, 1961, present an objective account of his work and his observations.

7. Arthur Behrand, gunner officer, wrote two books about his war experiences – *Make Me a Soldier*, 1961 and *As From Kemmel Hill*, 1963, both published by Eyre & Spottiswood.

8. Colonel Fuller was one of the great advocates and exponents of tanks. He reached the rank of Major-General and became a leading military historian and analyst. This comment comes from his *Memoirs of an Unconventional Soldier*, Eyre & Spottiswood, 1936.

9. From a letter in the archives of the Australian War Memorial, quoted by Bill Gammage in *The Broken Years*, Penguin, 1975.

10. W.S. Churchill, *The World Crisis, 1914–1918*; referred to in other Chapter notes.

11. Lord Esher had great political influence through his friendship with King Edward VII, George V and many leading statesmen. He never held an important office but liked the indirect exercise of power. This extract is from his *Journals and Letters*, 1920.

12. Brigadier-General J.H. Edmonds, op. cit.

13. Bean, op. cit.

14. Basil Liddell Hart was a trenchant critic of the Allied conduct of World War I. This extract is from his *The Real War 1914–18*, published in 1930 and, in 1970, as *History of the First World War*.

15. W.H.A. ('Archie') Groom wrote his memoirs of the war in *Poor Bloody Infantry: The Truth Untold*, Kimber, 1976, Picardy, 1983.

Statements by generals are from official reports, unit war diaries, despatches or official histories.

10

TRIUMPH at CAMBRAI

Disaster at Cambrai

Third Ypres had dragged to a muddy and bloody end but the generals had not finished with 1917. Throughout the year the future of tanks in the war had occupied the minds of their supporters and, equally, those of their denigrators. Among the latter was General Kiggell, Haig's Chief-of-Staff, who did his considerable best to limit their use. He was among those who considered that the order for a thousand tanks, placed after the use of the machines at Flers, was absurd and he played a part in inducing the Army Council to cancel the order. The ever watchful Lloyd George cancelled the cancellation.

CIGS, General Robertson, was another who campaigned against tanks. Liddell Hart says the main opponents of tanks were not the Germans but GHQ in France. In one of the most biting, cynical criticisms ever made about the General Staff, he writes,[1] 'Let it be said to the credit of those who opposed the tank that if they had not the ingenuity to devise means of beating the Germans they were fertile in devices to beat the sponsors of the tank.'

One man they tried to beat was Major Albert Stern, who was in charge of tank production. The War Office ordered him to cancel an order for 1,000 tanks of a new model. This alarmed Stern, who was fortunate enough to be a temporary soldier with an independent income in the City. He went direct to Lloyd George and found that he had not given approval for the cancellation. Stern then confronted General Robertson and told him that he had Lloyd George's authority not to carry out the cancellation. His courage saved the future of the tank but Stern and others of like mind were removed from their posts at the Ministry of Munitions. Stern himself was replaced by an Admiral who had never seen a tank and could therefore be counted on not to worry the generals about building them. This was wilful and malicious bungling.

Colonel J.F.C. Fuller, the chief Tank Staff Officer, produced a pamphlet on tank tactics and stressed the advantages of surprise and a short bombardment when using them. GHQ favoured neither a short bombardment nor tanks and had the pamphlet withdrawn. Colonel E.D. Swinton also ran foul of GHQ. As Tank Commander he was held responsible and dismissed for the scruffiness and indiscipline which GHQ detected in tank crews. Staff officers complained that the tank men were always so dirty. Had they ventured inside the primitive, dark, oily and smelly tanks they would have found it was impossible to stay clean for more then a few minutes. To replace the incomparable Swinton, GHQ brought in General Anley, who was ordered to establish discipline among tank crews. When starting his job Anley announced that he 'was not interested in tanks', thus echoing Kiggell, who had appointed him.

The original concept for a large-scale tank raid had come from the fertile mind of Colonel Fuller. Bravely disregarding the sensitivities of duller minds at GHQ, Fuller, on 3 August 1917, produced a plan and in so doing announced that, 'From a tank point of view the Third Battle of Ypres may be considered dead. To go on using tanks in the present conditions will not only lead to good machines and better personnel being thrown away, but also to a loss of morale in the infantry and tank crews. From an infantry point of view, the Third Battle of Ypres may be considered comatose. It can only be continued at colossal loss and little gain.' Not surprisingly, Fuller was not a favourite with Haig and his GHQ staff.

Fuller proposed the capture of St Quentin, 'to restore British prestige and strike a theatrical blow against Germany before the

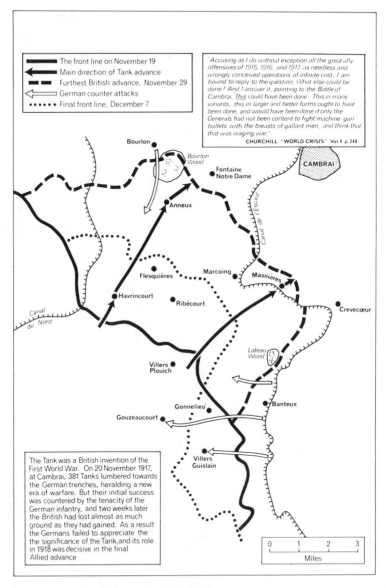

The front line on November 19
Main direction of Tank advance
Furthest British advance, November 29
German counter attacks
Final front line, December 7

"Accusing as I do without exception all the great ally offensives of 1915, 1916, and 1917, as needless and wrongly conceived operations of infinite cost, I am bound to reply to the question. What else could be done? And I answer it, pointing to the Battle of Cambrai. This could have been done. This in many variants, this in larger and better forms ought to have been done, and would have been done if only the Generals had not been content to fight machine-gun bullets with the breasts of gallant men, and think that that was waging war."

CHURCHILL "WORLD CRISIS" Vol. 4 p. 348

Bourlon
Bourlon Wood
CAMBRAI
Fontaine Notre Dame
Anneux
Canal de l'Escaut
Marcoing
Flesquières
Masnières
Havrincourt
Ribécourt
Crevecœur
Canal du Nord
Lateau Wood
Villers Plouich
Gonnelieu
Banteux
Gouzeaucourt
Villers Guislain

The Tank was a British invention of the First World War. On 20 November 1917, at Cambrai, 381 Tanks lumbered towards the German trenches, heralding a new era of warfare. But their initial success was countered by the tenacity of the German infantry, and two weeks later the British had lost almost as much ground as they had gained. As a result the Germans failed to appreciate the the significance of the Tank, and its role in 1918 was decisive in the final Allied advance

0   1   2   3
Miles

Tanks: a new method of attack, 1917–1918

winter.' When this idea was not backed, Fuller produced a detailed plan for a tank 'raid' south of Cambrai. In the space of 8 to 12 hours he wanted to 'destroy, demoralise and disorganise, not capture ground.' As Fuller stressed, 'The essence of the entire operation is surprise and rapidity of movement.'

Fuller and his colleagues chose the rolling downland, west of Cambrai, where the ground was still relatively firm and green. The German line was known to be lightly manned at the point of attack and the tank men believed that the machines could smash a large breech for infantry and cavalry.

General Byng liked the idea but wanted something grander than a raid, no matter how big it might be. He proposed nothing less than a breakthrough attack to capture Cambrai. The project was shelved, largely because Kiggell convinced Haig that it was a mistake to attack at Cambrai while the Ypres battle was going on. Haig, who still saw the tank as only 'a minor factor', was easily turned against the Cambrai project.

In mid-October, when it was too late to help the push in the Salient, the tank attack idea was revived and sanctioned for November. It was now to be a full-scale battle conducted by Byng, with the Tank Corps playing an important role. Byng's plan was too ambitious for the infantry he had available, just six divisions for the initial attack, and none at all as reserves – at least not near to the area.

Byng agreed to do without a preliminary bombardment, for the sake of surprise. The Tank Staff brought all their tanks into position by night and hid them by day so that enemy fliers would not spot them.

Of the 474 Mark I tanks available for the task, 376 were fighting tanks; the others were equipped for supply, communications or wire demolition. Byng proposed to attack on a 6-mile front and capture the ridges of Flesquieres and Bourlon. Cavalry would then sweep through to capture Cambrai from the Germans. After this, six infantry divisions, with others in support, as well as cavalry, tanks and guns would attack northeast and roll up the German front. Haig told Byng that he had 48 hours to achieve some significant gain otherwise he would call off the attack.

On the night of 19 November the tank crews prepared for combat, tying onto the nose of each machine a fascine – an enormous and weighty bundle of logs and brushwood as broad as the tank and 6 feet or more in diameter. The fascines would be dropped into the enemy trenches to form a rough 'bridge' by which the tank could cross. In earlier usage tanks had ditched in trenches or straddled them and were unable to continue.

At 6.10 a.m. on 20 November Brigadier-General Hugh Elles, GOC Tank Corps, in his command tank 'Hilda', led forward 381 machines in the first major tank operation in history. As they reached the German trenches the female tanks turned at right angles and moved along the parados to machine-gun the Germans who came rushing out of their dugouts. Every third tank dropped a fascine in the first trench. Other tanks, crossing the same bridge, rumbled on to drop their fascines in the second and third trenches, respectively.

Some tanks, as prearranged, crushed through the wire defences; others, fitted with grapnels, dragged the wire away so that cavalry could penetrate. Byng's infantry followed close behind the tanks and quickly captured one position after another from the demoralised Germans.

The large number and unexpected appearance of the tanks, as well as their fearsome nature shocked the Germans. As the giant machines crushed in the sides of their trenches many ran or surrendered. This was understandable for there had never been such a sight on any battlefield. Even veteran German soldiers panicked.

The first phase was a tremendous success. Ludendorff, who heard the news about 8 a.m., ordered an immediate counter-attack. Back at British GHQ the Staff could barely believe that the impossible had happened – a breakthrough!

As yet, nobody knew that Lieut.-General Sir Montague ('Uncle') Harper, GOC 51st Highland Division, was sabotaging the operation. Harper, educated at Bath College, was only fifty-two, but reactionary to the point of imbecility. Stubborn and with tunnel vision, he had led the 51st since 1915, yet not until mid-1917 had he come around to the idea that perhaps the machine-gun was a useful weapon. His late arrival at this conclusion may have cost many of his men their lives.

He still 'disapproved' of tanks and had given his division no training in working in collaboration with them. True, the men had had some training in tactics, but it was contrary to that advised by the Tank Corps. For 'Uncle' the entire Cambrai plan was 'most fantastic and unmilitary scheme'. He was convinced that the Hindenburg Line could not be captured at the time specified in the plan – so he delayed his assault by 1 hour.

Specifically, the tanks crossed the Hindenburg Line at 8.30 a.m. but Harper refused to follow until 9.30. All around him was the clear need to *move*, but 'Uncle' stayed put. During that hour the Germans rushed field guns into Flesquieres Ridge. As the tanks climbed the ridge and became silhouetted the gunners opened fire at short range and one by one the tanks were hit, 16 in all on Harper's front, and not a single Tank Corps man survived. A handful of German machine-guns blocked the advance of Harper's entire division.

The hold-up at Flesquieres blunted the attack's momentum. Three divisions of cavalry, waiting to gallop through the expected gap, did not get through. This was not altogether 'Uncle' Harper's fault. The cavalry commanders on the spot were unable to act on the evidence of their eyes but had to wait for orders from a HQ far behind the fighting.

Having waited with gallant impatience for years for a chance to prove their mettle, the four cavalry divisions – with the exception of the Canadian Fort Garry Horse – did nothing but look decorative. It was not the men's fault; they lacked senior leadership. Six hours after the barbed wire had been cleared for them, the horsemen went through. They were too late.

GHQ and Third Army HQ had not arranged for adequate infantry reinforcements to exploit any breakthroughs, so the spectacular success of the Tank Corps was not exploited. Nor had they permitted Elles and Fuller to keep an adequate tank reserve.

Nevertheless, the success was real enough. Two German divisions had been broken, more than 8,000 soldiers were captured, a few thousand more were killed or wounded. Scores of machine-guns and even a few field guns were captured. British killed or wounded totalled 4,000, low figures for the time. When news of the success reached Britain church bells were rung for the only time in the war. Allied leaders sent their congratulations.

To the tune of 'Byng! Byng! Byng!' a New York newspaper devoted an entire column to the victory:

> You are the thing, the whole thing, Byng, Byng;
> You sent them on the wing, Byng, Byng.
> You made the Boches' ears sing, Byng, Byng,
> And the Kaiser's too to ring, Byng.
> You'll take your rank, Byng, with the first in the hearts
> Of those who do their parts, Byng, Byng.
> And all along the Front they'll hail you King Byng
> Of all the British Tommies from every clime
> 'Twas all sublime . . . etc.

The *London Daily Mail* republished this doggeral on 24 November. It might well have been given the title *The Battle of Cambrai – Earlier Stages*.

Any belief that Byng's battle was decisive was short-lived. At the end of 20 November, 179 tanks were out of action, many through mechanical troubles or getting stuck in trenches. All the others had been in action for 16 hours and needed maintenance and fresh crews. Denied reserve tanks before the battle, Elles and Fuller could only regroup the machines they still had.

Haig had said he would give the attack 48 hours to succeed. At that time the British held Flesquieres Ridge but the Germans still clung to Bourlon Ridge, which guarded the north-western approaches to Cambrai. The British 111 Corps on the right had stopped advancing. German divisions, rushed from Flanders and the Aisne River front, reached the Cambrai sector. Haig decided to hold the ground won and to advance but German resistance was stubborn and at Cambrai a German officer knocked out five tanks single-handed until he was killed.

On 26 November the tanks which had been in action with IV Corps were withdrawn for refitting, but the infantry struggle for

Bourion Ridge continued. Crown Prince Rupprecht, the German sector commander, massed 20 divisions to attack the flanks of the salient won by the British and thus cut off Byng's forward force. Ludendorff agreed with him that it was a splendid opportunity and Rupprecht struck with General von Marwitz's Second Army on 30 November. Third Army HQ had known that the Germans were massing – scouting fliers frequently reported the large enemy movements – but the Staff issued no instructions and did not order the tanks back to the front. When the Germans attacked with great force and spirit Byng's position soon became desperate. One of his divisions, the 12th, broke and fled.

The Guards Division was rushed from reserve and fought magnificently in a counter-attack. Colonel Fuller heard about the German onslaught when he was in the middle of supervising entrainment of his tanks to the rear. He ordered forward every tank that would still run – 63 of them – and they fought an action as gallant as that of 20 November.

However, on the night of 4 December Haig felt that he had no option but to order a withdrawal to the old British lines. The battle ended without any overall British gain of territory. The British suffered 43,000 casualties, of whom 6,000 were prisoners taken on the first day of the German counter-offensive, and 158 guns. German losses were 41,000, including 11,000 captured, and 138 guns.

Recriminations flew like missiles in every direction and a hunt for scapegoats took place. In London, Haig's reputation suffered badly and the War Cabinet demanded an explanation for the failure which had overtaken a victory. Byng made a report which Haig endorsed hoping that this would end the matter. The Third Army had not been taken by suprise, Byng said; the fault lay with the junior officers, NCOs and men who had failed to stop the German breakthrough on 30 November.

Not satisfied with this explanation, the politicians asked Byng why he had not sent reinforcements to that part of the line which was under most pressure and which finally gave way. None had been asked for, said Byng, but in any case he and his staff had not considered that further troops were necessary. These were lies but Haig endorsed them and added that the senior commanders were in no way to blame.

The War Cabinet called in the South African General, Jan Christian Smuts, to adjudicate. The choice of the pro-Establishment Smuts gave notice that a cover-up was imminent. Following his deliberations, Smuts announced that High Command Army and Corps command were not to blame; they had done all that might be expected to meet any German attack. The fault lay with local commanders who might have lost their heads or with junior officers, NCOs and men. Smuts stated that he preferred this latter explanation.

'Uncle' Harper escaped censure for his mishandling of the 51st Highland Division on 20 November in an ingenious way. He claimed that a German gunner officer had, single-handedly, destroyed all the tanks on the ridge in front of him. There was nothing that Harper could have done to save them. Members of his division went along with this falsehood, possibly out of shame for not being up with the tanks to deal with the German guns, at the moment when they were vulnerable to infantry attack. In fact, at the point that Harper could have intervened, only five tanks had been hit.

Byng resolved his embarrassment by sacking two of his Corps commanders. Such a decisive action had the psychological effect of convincing the critics that Byng himself was 'obviously' not at fault.

Haig, Byng, Kiggell, Harper, the cavalry commanders, the various Staffs, all must share the blame for final failure of Cambrai.

'Stupidity does not explain the behaviour of these generals,' says Norman Dixon.[1] 'So great was their fear of loss of self-esteem, and so imperative their need for social approval, that they could resort to tactics beyond the reach of any self-respecting "donkey". From their shameless self-interest, lack of loyalty to their subordinates and apparent indifference to the verdict of posterity, a picture emerges of personalities deficient in something other than intellectual acumen.'

Principles, perhaps?

TRIUMPH AT CAMBRAI

Bryan Cooper[2] says, 'And so the whitewashing went on, to protect generals who in the main had little conception of what the front line was like – and no intention of going there to find out.' One of those infantrymen so blamed was J.H. Everest. During the 2 days when he and his fellow soldiers were being pushed back by the Germans they had no water to drink and no food to eat. At the end of the second day, while waiting in a trench for a renewed attack, Everest went up to his company commander and asked for permission to search for water. 'My request was refused,' Everest wrote later. 'Nevertheless, I went over the top and found some water in a mud-hole, thus ending two days of torture.' Shortly afterwards Everest was wounded and found himself in the Australian General Hospital at Abbeville. But the most bitter pill of all on top of all this 'was to be blamed for the commanders' mistakes.'

Haig assumed the whole responsibility – but also sent home several subordinate commanders. It was a clever move. Simultaneously, he 'did the decent thing' by accepting the traditional responsibility of high command, while proving that he was not, in fact, responsible.

Lloyd George more than ever distrusted Haig's strategy. Privately, he referred to Haig as 'wooden-fisted, club-footed, and without imagination.'[3]

For his part, Haig was intent on yet another great British offensive and agreed with CIGS Robertson on the 'impossibility of working with such a man' as Lloyd George.

Haig's Chief of Intelligence, John Charteris, was peeved by the failure of the Cambrai initiative:

It really was, in its conception and execution a very fine affair. To undertake a new battle was the last development the enemy expected of us; and to do what is absolutely unexpected is to do the big thing in war. The British command suddenly attacked the Germans in their strongest part of the Hindenburg Line. Their line was particularly strong at this point. It was more than annoying to think that just when we had successfully solved the problem of a breakthrough we had not the means, owing to commitments elsewhere, to push the thrust home. I do not think that the skill of generalship and organisation that [Cambrai] showed were quite appreciated.

Charteris, writing in 1920, was pushing the GHQ line. His statement is full of false self-congratulation, specious statements and downright untruths. The execution of the plan was anything but a fine affair, except for that part of it which lay in the hands of the Tank Corps commanders. Charteris extolled the advantages of doing the 'absolutely unexpected' but at GHQ such tactics were as rare as compassion. The planning for surprise on 20 November was again to the credit of the Tank Corps, though Byng agreed to the scheme. Contrary to Charteris' claims, the British did *not* attack a 'particularly strong' part of the German line and would have been guilty of criminal folly had they knowingly done so. It was, in fact, a weak part of the enemy line. Charteris says that GHQ did not have the means to 'push the thrust home'. The means for victory were available but they were not used. At the time there were no special 'commitments elsewhere' as the rest of the British front was quiet. Charteris complains that 'skill of generalship' was not properly appreciated. Certain men demonstrated this skill – Elles and Fuller among them – but they were not in high command, as Charteris wants his readers to assume.

The greater bungling at Cambrai occurred on 20 November, the day of the tank attack. Had the operation remained a great tank raid, as in Fuller's plan, it would almost certainly have been an unqualified success. Thus it would have done much to restore British morale after the agony of Third Ypres and it must have damaged German morale. But since it was, after all, a break-through battle it should have been much better planned. Haig and Byng and their staff knew that should they drive a salient into the German front they would need as many as 40 divisons just to hold it, let alone expand it. But only a few reserve divisions were available and they were too far off. The German counter-offensive of 30 November–4 December was the direct result of what happened on 20 November.

In her book Lady Haig skated around the disaster of Cambrai, but said that the decision to abandon the Bourlon Wood positions was taken to save the loss of further British lives. Haig may have used this as an excuse to justify withdrawal which was, indeed, essential.

The final word on Cambrai may be left to Winston Churchill:[5]

> Accusing as I do without exception all the great allied offensives of 1915, 1916 and 1917 as needless and wrongly conceived operations of infinite cost, I am bound to reply to the question, What else could be done? And I answer it, pointing to the Battle of Cambrai. 'This could have been done.' This in many variants, this in larger and better forms ought to have been done, and would have been done if only the Generals had not been content to fight machine-gun bullets with the breasts of gallant men, and think that that was waging war.

While this book is not concerned with German bungling, it must be said that the German military leaders also bungled over Cambrai. They saw the success of the British tanks but learnt nothing from it. Throughout the war the Germans no more than experimented with tanks.

NOTES

1. Professor Norman Dixon, *The Psychology of Military Incompetence*, op cit.
2. Bryan Cooper, *The Ironclads of Cambrai*, London, 1967.
3. Quoted by Tim Travers in *The Killing Ground*, Allen & Unwin, 1987.
4. Brigadier-General John Charteris, Haig's Chief of Intelligence, *At GHQ*, op cit.
5. Winston Churchill, *The World Crisis 1911–1918*, op cit.

11

GERMAN BREAK-THROUGHS

A Better Way to Attack

The year 1918 is sometimes presented as 'a year of victory' – that is, Allied victory – but this description is misleading. The Allies were victorious at the end of 1918, but this should not be taken to mean that British senior leadership improved during the year. While some generals were demonstrating the benefits of enterprise and initiative and showing consideration for their fighting men they were relatively junior in the complex hierarchy of military command.

The first half of 1918 on the Western Front was a period of almost unrelieved disaster for the Allied command, with British and French generals equally incompetent. Some blunders were so great that they verged on the catastrophic.

Generalship was much more competent in Palestine, where Allenby, having been little more than a mediocre general in France, proved himself a master of mobile open warfare. His campaigns succeeded and his career prospered largely through the work of three of his subordinate generals. They were Lieut.-General Sir P.W. Chetwode, GOC Desert Column, Lieut.-General Sir Harry Chauvel, GOC Australian Light Horse and Brigadier-General E.W.C. Chaytor, GOC New Zealand Mounted Rifles. Chauvel was the finest cavalry general of the century and his Australian Light Horse was astonishingly successful. These troopers fought 36 battles against the Turks in 30 months and won all of them.

Allenby was to lose 60,000 of his best men, mostly infantry, as reinforcements for the mincing machine which was operating on the Western Front.

Germany started 1918 with a psychological advantage because, on 3 December 1917, Bolshevik Russia signed an armistice. As a minor bonus for the Germans, Rumania, which had come in on the Allied side, collapsed. The Eastern Front campaigns had kept masses of German troops pinned down; now they could be hurried to the Western Front.

On the debit side for Germany, food was short because of the success of the Allied naval blockade. Turkey, Austria-Hungary and Bulgaria were weakening. Intelligence reports before the German General Staff showed that American military strength was building up by tens of thousands of men each week.

Hindenburg and Ludendorff realised the pressing need to use the early months of 1918 for offensive action before the American weight became too great. A genuine student of war, Ludendorff analysed the campaigns on Germany's Western and Eastern fronts. The stalemate on the West, he concluded, was the result of lack of surprise. British and French attacks had failed again and again, and from where Ludendorff stood behind the powerful German defences the cause was obvious. On every occasion, other than Cambrai, the Allies had announced their intention to attack by bombarding the German positions. Thus warned, the Germans were ready to meet the assault. In German understanding, the British had failed at Cambrai because they had given the Germans time to bring up reinforcements, thus they had forfeited surprise.

The German official histories record that the High Command received from Intelligence sources copies of British reports concerning the campaigns of 1917. The historian says, 'Haig's despatches dealing with the attacks of 1917 were found most valuable, because they showed how not to do it.'

Reversing the usual order of priorities, Ludendorff put tactics before strategy. It was pointless, he told his General Staff, to have strategic objectives unless tactics could achieve a breakthrough. From the moment that a breakthrough occurred strategy could be adapted to fit the circumstances. He would do what the British and French had so starkly failed to do – achieve surprise. With a massive attack he would hit his enemy with gas and shellfire before they could organise themselves.

German experience against the Russian armies was also brought into use. Ludendorff ordered his generals to rid their minds of the old-fashioned idea of infantry attacking in waves according to a rigid plan. Machine-gun scouting teams would be the front attackers. Their mission was to find weak points in the enemy line. Having located them, the machine-gunners would fire signal flares to call their infantry to those points. It was a clever and simple idea. If German machine-gun fire failed to produce an Allied response at any one point, then there was the weak place which the Germans sought.

The pace would be set by the fastest units, not the slowest – as was usual – and no effort would be made to keep a uniform alignment. In places where British troops might hold out they were to be bypassed and dealt with later. In any case, once bypassed, they might well surrender. To ensure rapid flow of information back to GHQ and Army HQs, Ludendorff ordered that small reconnaissance parties would be detailed solely to send back news.

The Germans carefully trained their divisions in the tactics which General von Hutier had so successfully developed at Riga. The troops were taught to forget all that they had so painfully learned about trench warfare and to adapt themselves to mobility. The new pattern of attack consisted of short intensive artillery preparations, a creeping barrage, bypassing of enemy strongpoints, massive infiltration and continued forward movement.

The British and French almost invariably attacked the Germans' strongest lines. Ludendorff proposed to strike where the Allied line was, by German Intelligence estimates, the weakest. The sector decided on was 47 miles of the front held by the British

5th Army under Gough and the Third Army under Byng. The front extended from south of the Somme River north to Arras.

Meanwhile, in London, Lloyd George and his supporters were trying to find a strategy of their own to reduce Haig's propensity and opportunity for ruinous offensives. The Prime Minister knew that he could not rid himself of Haig as a Commander-in-Chief because he had the king's total backing. However, Haig's principal supporter in London, Robertson the CIGS, was vulnerable. Lloyd George believed that if he could remove Robertson the War Cabinet could more easily control Haig. He was already afraid that Haig intended to repeat in 1918 his 'hammering offensives' of 1917. Haig was confident of his own power base. During discussions over the formation of an allied Supreme War Council, to be based at Versailles, he explained to Lloyd George that only the Army Council, acting through the CIGS, or a Field-Marshal senior to himself, could give him orders.

The Cabinet had not only decided to remove Robertson but to take from any future CIGS the responsibility for issuing the orders of the government in regard to military operations. This would prevent the CIGS and the Commander-in-Chief from forming too close a military relationship. Lloyd George told Haig that he was contemplating the appointment of General Sir Henry Wilson as CIGS, while Robertson would go to Versailles as the British military representative on the Supreme War Council. Haig objected, saying that Wilson was distrusted and unpopular in the army. He meant that he personally did not like Wilson, who had been GOC IV Corps in 1915–16. Lloyd George saw an opening in Haig's dislike of Wilson as CIGS and suggested that Haig himself should come back from the Western Front to be generalissimo of all British forces. Haig sidestepped this trap by saying that as he expected a German attack a sudden change at the front would be unwise.

Robertson refused to go to Versailles and was given a home command. Lloyd George offered the post of CIGS to Plumer, who also refused it. Wilson then accepted it and Rawlinson went as military representative to Versailles. Lloyd George survived the political crisis which all of these machinations had produced with the satisfaction of knowing that he had split Robertson and Haig. Wilson was the Prime Minister's man, not the Commander-in-Chief's lackey.

Haig was also now without the dubious help of Kiggell as his Chief of General Staff. After his first visit to the front at Passchendaele, which shocked him, Kiggell broke down with 'nervous exhaustion' and left the comfort of the chateau at Montreuil for home. Haig lamented his departure. 'I am very loth [sic] to part with Kigg's help and sound advice,' he wrote. The American historian, H.H. Herwig,[1] finds Haig's distress at losing Kiggell 'incredible'. Posted to Guernsey as Lieutenant Governor and military head, Kiggell was in no position to further hinder the British war effort. He was replaced as CGS by Lieut.-General Sir Herbert Lawrence. This was rapid promotion since Lawrence had only a few weeks earlier succeeded Brigadier-General Charteris as Haig's Chief of Intelligence. Charteris had been partly responsible for Haig's blunders because he had been feeding him with the type of information which he knew Haig preferred, such as reports that German morale was breaking.

Haig always alleged that Lloyd George directly denied him the large reinforcements he called for. Had he been given more manpower, he claimed, he could have achieved victory more rapidly. Edmonds' Official History supports Haig's claims and it is known that Winston Churchill told Edmonds of Lloyd George's remark that he 'was not going to be Haig's butcher'. More recently, however, David Woodward[2] has argued that it was Robertson, CIGS, with War Office backing, who held the reserves in Britain. In one way Haig had only himself to blame as he had assured Robertson that even in the worst situation he could hold his lines for 18 days, thus allowing time for the reserves to arrive. During and after Robertson's period as CIGS it was Lloyd George's policy to attempt to check Haig's mania for the offensive by controlling manpower, but he did not block reinforcements needed to make good natural wastage. Haig had himself done the damage to his prospects for 1918 by squandering 400,000 men in the 1917 offensive.

With British morale low in the winter of 1917–18, Deputy

GERMAN BREAKTHROUGHS

Chaplain-General Gwynne proposed to Haig that a card should be prepared to state the objectives of the war and distributed to the troops. It read:

> Better homes where the children can grow up healthy and strong; better education which gives a child full opportunity for developing the faculties implanted in him by God; a fair deal for labour, giving to the worker a fuller life; justice for women and a resolute stand against prostitution; a discipline which keeps a man at his best and maintains holy matrimony as the ideal of family life.

We can only speculate about how the troops would have received this high-minded prose. Most of the cards were captured before distribution by the Germans when they broke through in March.

While Ludendorff plotted his great spring offensives – he had five separate strikes in mind – Lieut.-General Sir Ivor Maxse, GOC XVIII Corps, became uneasy and circulated a forecast of an impending 'Storm Trooper' type of attack. GHQ ignored his prediction but within a month it was to be proved brilliantly accurate. General Gough was also apprehensive and on 1 February he sent a signal to GHQ saying that he expected to be attacked. He gave his reasons. One was that he had received information that General von Hutier, with the 18th German Army under his command, had been transferred to the area opposite the Fifth Army front. General von Hutier had a formidable reputation as an offensive-minded and clever general. In September 1917 he had waged a successful offensive to capture Riga from the Russians. Also, Gough reported that many new German aerodromes and extra bridges over the St Quentin–Cambrai Canal indicated preparations for an offensive.

GHQ did not give Gough a definite order to blow up certain causeways and bridges over which the Germans would advance but then he should not have needed an order. He could do as he wished on his own front.

The British 5th and 3rd army combined front was 70 miles; Gough had 47 miles of it. His Fifth Army front had fewer men and guns per mile than any other section of the British line. The reserves behind it were spaced to provide only one division for every 18,000 yards of the front, whereas on the Third Army front there was reserve division for 8,000 yards.

Gough asked for more labour and stores, more Royal Engineers, and more detailed intelligence reports. Haig blundered in refusing to provide the labour to build a strong defensive line behind the old Somme battlefields.

Evidence of German intentions became increasingly plain. On 16 February Haig came to the personal conclusion that a strong attack would hit his front between the Oise and the Scarpe rivers. On 10 March the routine GHQ intelligence summary repeated that a major attack, with little warning, would be made on the Arras–St Quentin sector. On 17 March this Intelligence view remained unchanged. On 18 and 19 March prisoners and deserters on the Third and Fifth army fronts gave information that an offensive was imminent. Gough stressed to GHQ his anxiety about his army's front but Haig spoke about inflicting a heavy defeat on the Germans. He was only worried that the German High Command might *not* attack, on the grounds that the British front was so very strong.

In March 1917 the Allies had had 178 divisions confronting the Germans 129. Now, a year later, the German High Command had a slight numerical advantage and as more and more troops were brought from the Russian front this advantage increased. Ludendorff had three experienced armies available for the 'Michael' offensive – von Bulow's 17th, refreshed and reinforced since its victory at Caporetto on the Italian front, the 2nd, and von Hutier's 18th from the Eastern Front.

Operation 'Michael' opened on 21 March. Following a short but violent bombardment, 62 divisions advanced against 26 British divisions. In the mist and smoke, the new German tactic of infiltration in strength was instantly successful in the south. In the woods and valleys of the Somme, British Corps and Divisional HQs quickly gained the impression that the Germans were outflanking them, whereas in fact they were being massively infiltrated.

Many HQs unnecessarily rushed to the rear where they believed they could control events more efficiently. Totally rigid in its defence training, the British army could not adapt to the infiltration tactics. The British messily retreated when they should have withdrawn in an orderly, disciplined way, with their guns intact.

The right of Gough's army swung back, leaving the way open for the Germans to press forward to Compiegne and Paris. On the British right, French troops fought to plug the gap, but on 27 March the Germans captured Montdidier, alarmingly close to Paris. Gough's army retreated daily and on its northern front was pressed back towards the vital centre of Amiens. By 30 March the Germans had captured 80,000 prisoners and 975 guns.

It was during this period that General ('Uncle') Harper, with the bad memories of Cambrai behind him, came back into battle. He had recently been appointed GOC IV Corps, part of which was his old division, the 51st. The 51st did not try to make a stand against the German thrust but each day pulled back, in what Tim Travers[3] calls a 'dour, deliberate and selfish retreat.' Harper appeared unable to impose his own will on the 51st. At a divisional commanders' crisis conference on 25 March the 51st's general refused to put his division in the line. Harper should at once have removed this general and replaced him but failed to. IV Corps HQ was under great pressure and reports were confused but Harper could have been much more decisive.

Somebody had to take the blame for the British collapse and Gough was the obvious victim. But he was sacked 2 years too late and for the wrong reasons. It was ironic that the man who had deserved dismissal for mishandling his part of the Somme offensive in 1916 and for his pig-headed stupidity in the Passchendaele offensive in 1917 should be fired for the one job he did well. Gough was never better than during the retreat, showing calmness, courage and bouyancy under incredibly difficult circumstances. He set a good example and fought his delaying battles as well as anyone could have done.

Unfortunately for him, the distrust he had earned during 1916 and 1917 made his subordinates, colleagues and allies distrust him in 1918 and it was this, as much as anything else, which brought about his dismissal. Rawlinson succeeded him in command of the 5th Army.

Haig had telegraphed to London suggesting that the CIGS should come to GHQ France to discuss the serious tactical situation. Now, concerned about changes in French strategy, he asked not only the CIGS but the Secretary of State for War, Lord Derby, to come to France. On 25 March he requested them by telegram to arrange that 'General Foch or some other determined general who would fight, should be given supreme command in France.' The following day Foch was appointed to co-ordinate all Allied operations on the Western Front and a week later he was given the 'strategic direction of military operations'. This did not, however, give him any direct control over the British Army.

On 28 March Ludendorff's divisions attacked north and south of Arras but many of his best assault troops had been killed or wounded and this part of his offensive ceased on 5 April. He had not won a strategic victory despite having captured 90,000 prisoners, 1,100 guns and immense quantities of stores.

The Germans were stopped not by superior staff work or by any particularly good generalship, but by the dour courage of the troops well led at lower levels. The units of the much maligned 5th Army rallied and then stood firm.

Ludendorff had established the principle of following the line of least Allied resistance but now, in a serious blunder, he broke his own principle. He should have massed his reserves to exploit the southern breakthrough. Instead, he checked his thrusting 18th Army while trying with other forces to capture Arras. The 18th Army, as ordered, sat tight for 2 days – just long enough for French reserves to close the breach.

British blunders at high level assisted Ludendorff and the German General Staff in their next offensive, 'George 1', which was informally renamed 'Georgette' because many fewer troops were used than had been originally planned. Haig's GHQ, as well as General Sir Henry Horne, GOC First Army, had plenty of intelligence that a major attack was likely – and imminent – across the lowlands of the Lys river valley, on the southern

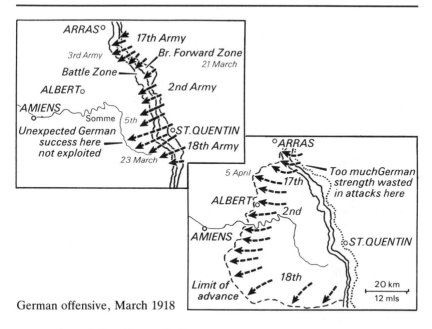

German offensive, March 1918

extremity of the Ypres Salient.

The Germans went to no pains whatever to mask their imminent attack – in marked contrast to their 'Michael' offensive. They were too intent on speed. From 31 March, British fliers reported continual enemy movements. On 1 April just one observer counted 55 trains within 2 hours, all moving along the lines supplying the Lys front. Horne's transport chief told him that the Lys sector was not only the most probable point of attack but the only such point.

Yet, on 7 April GHQ was convinced of an imminent attack on Vimy Ridge, much further south than the Lys river, despite air reports and air photographs which revealed that German troops were being withdrawn from the Vimy sector. Haig convinced himself that Ludendorff *should* attack Vimy Ridge, because it was the strongest part of the British front. After all, Haig had attacked Ludendorff's strongest front at Passchendaele.

While GHQ and Horne's HQ deluded themselves, reports kept coming in not only from air observers but ground patrols that enemy strength was growing alarmingly opposite the Portuguese. Reliable junior officers saw German soldiers carrying ammunition into the enemy's support trenches, a sure sign of an impending attack. The GOC 51st Division suggested to First Army HQ that he should move his men into the strong trenches behind the Portuguese; his request was turned down. Horne's 'Q' staff advised the preparation of emergency supply dumps 15 miles in the rear, ready for any enemy breakthrough. This request was also rejected but the 'Q' staff ignored Horne and did the job anyway. The dumps helped to meet the crisis.

On 9 April Ludendorff set 'Georgette' in motion. The place and time had been well chosen. Two weak Portuguese divisions were holding the trenches on the Lys River front. They were due to be relieved by British divisions within 24 hours, so Ludendorff's timing had little margin for error. The Portuguese, who were boastfully overconfident and lamentably led, did not have their heart in the war and bolted. They did not stop until they reached the coast, 15 miles away.

The way was open for a major German drive towards the Channel ports. Within 2 days the British position was so desperate that on the night of 11–12 April Haig issued an order which was almost instantly famous:

> Many amongst us are now tired. To those I would say that victory will belong to the side which holds out the longest. The French army is moving rapidly and in great force to our support. There is no other course open to us but to fight it out. With our backs to the wall and believing in the justice of our cause, each one of us must fight on to the end.

The order makes an interesting study for it is not what it seems to be. The thought that the side which could hold out the longest would win expresses Haig's constant military philosophy. It was virtually his doctrine. Implicit in 'holding out' for a lengthy period is the H.C.I. fixation. In confessing that no other course was open to him, Haig, on this occasion, was telling the literal truth. He had nothing left in reserve, no fallback plan. 'Fighting on to the end' carries with it his implicit resignation that the end is nigh. In such a critical situation any commander might be justified in assuring his desperate troops that help is on the way, but Haig was none too sure that the French would get there. One reason for his appeal was that he suspected that his soldiers would have to hold on without French help.

Haig's 'Backs to the Wall' Order of the Day has been presented as heroic and inspirational. It was neither. It was a rigid, dull and discouraging document. Paul Fussell[4] sees it as 'a dogged prohibition of manoeuvre or indeed of any tactics'. It was also self-indulgent and intended for a select senior readership, since Haig must have known that in the chaos of the time few soldiers would read it or hear it read. 'We never received it,' a corporal wrote. 'We to whom it was addressed, the infantry of the front line, were too scattered, too busy trying to survive, to be called into any formation to listen to orders of the day.'

Haig always had an eye on those who might judge him – such as the king – and it is possible that he framed his Order of the Day for them, since it tended to prove that under dire circumstances he had exhorted his soldiers to stand firm and to die, preferably facing the foe, in the best tradition of British arms.

On 13 April a soldier noted in his diary:[5]

A misty day was almost silent here but the strafe to the south kept breaking out. Our Divisional Ambulance arrangements being seemingly nil so far, the Australians on the right have agreed to clear us if necessary. An Anzac medical officer asked about the morale of this Division. Significant. Is every Anzac sick at the failure of the Imperial troops, as they call the BEF, to hold? Is the issue of rifles to the heavy artillery, coupled with a hint not to pull out so soon another time, a GHQ reflection on them or the infantry. The CinC tells us "our backs are to the wall". His men are asking, "Where's the bloody wall?"

Haig continued to urge Foch that the French army should take a greater part in the fighting, but no French troops moved into the line until 19 April. The Battle of the Lys raged for 3 weeks and took Prince Rupprecht's army 10 miles towards its goal. The Australian 1st Division did more to block the enemy advance than any other formation but with heavy casualties. The overall cost was enormous; the British 1st and 2nd Armies suffered 309,000 casualties.

The Germans attacked for another 2 weeks and on 25 April reached their high water mark with the capture of Kemmel Hill, close to Ypres. Ludendorff, short of divisions to carry out any more attacks with certainty of success, suspended the Lys offensive, but by now panic had set in at Allied HQ and Petain was preparing to defend Paris.

Lloyd George observed,[6] 'The Germans in a few days had broken through the allied line to a depth which the British and French offensives had never reached after weeks and months of laborious and costly effort. The prisoners and guns captured by the enemy in each of these offensives exceeded the highest record of the allies in any of their great offensives.'

The British position on the Western Front was more critical than the people at home were allowed to learn. Even in France certain facts were known only to those who had the greatest interest in keeping them secret. For instance, at the great base at Etaples near Boulogne, battalions of 17-year-olds were waiting for the birthday which would sent them up to the line. Middle-aged businessmen, some of them twice rejected in earlier years because of myopia and hernia, got through a final less demanding medical and, full of cheerful enthusiasm reached France. Many of them were dead within 48 hours.

Ludendorff's next offensive, 'Blucher', was targeted against the French. On 27 May, 15 divisions of Prince Wilhelm's army overwhelmed the two French divisions holding the Chemin des Dames line between Rheims and Soissons. On the first day sheer impetus took the Germans 13 miles and they reached the Marne river. The French lost 50,000 men taken prisoner, 600 guns and 2,000 machine-guns. Only Foch among the French generals kept his nerve and his confidence.

Ludendorff attempted to expand the great bulge of Rheims–Chateau Thierry–Soissons that he had punched in the French lines. Petain, the master of elastic defence, allowed the German flood to overrun his front lines and to batter itself to a standstill on a great semi-circular arc of well-prepared positions in rear areas.

Sir John Monash, the Australian Corps commander realised that it was possible to resolve the deadlock of trench warfare. Breaking away from the British H.C.I. fixation, the ghastly effects of which he had seen at close quarters during Third Ypres, Monash's solution was founded on the premise that infantrymen needed protection. He wrote,[7] 'The true role of infantry was not to expand itself upon heroic physical effort, not to wither away under merciless machine-gun fire, not to impale itself on hostile bayonets, but on the contrary, to advance under the maximum possible protection of the maximum possible array of mechanical resources, in the form of guns, machine-guns, tanks, mortars and aeroplanes.'

Monash tested his ideas in a relatively small operation at Hamel, on the Somme, on 4 July 1918. Infantry and tanks advanced in a predetermined method of co-operation, without a preliminary bombardment. Four carrier tanks took forward loads that would have needed 1,250 men to carry. For the first time on the Western Front aircraft were used to drop supplies onto the battlefield.

Other fliers were given reconnaissance duties. Equipped with maps identical to those being used by the infantry, each flying crew of pilot and observer was responsible for a small sector. Having marked enemy movements and the point of the Australian advance on a map, the observer dropped it to a motorcycle despatch rider at a designated point. In this way Monash and his staff had reliable information within minutes, and much more rapidly than that available to a commander in any previous battle.

Monash told his subordinates that they must not depart from his master plan. Should any German posts not fall at once they were to be kept under fire by a small number of men while the others bypassed them. The German positions were captured in 93 minutes, just 3 minutes more than the time Monash had allotted.

The Hamel victory has been credited to Rawlinson, since he was Monash's Army commander. But the operation was wholly Monash's in conception and execution and his troops were

Australian. A civil engineer in ordinary life, Monash was an amateur soldier with a highly professional outlook. The waste and incompetence which he had seen on the Western Front had sickened him. His capture of Hamel, and a few months later of Mont St Quentin and Peronne, proved that there was a better way to approach battles than the bludgeoning process used by the senior British commanders.

The principles used on 4 July were applied in planning the Battle of Amiens on 8 August, in which Monash advised Rawlinson. Rawlinson had 13 infantry divisions and 3 cavalry divisions, 2,070 guns, 800 aircraft and 540 tanks, consisting of 324 heavy Mark Vs, 96 lighter 'Whippets' and 120 supply tanks. The British forces were well supplied, largely because of Lloyd George's efforts to boost production that year.

Many precautions were taken to conceal the British dispositions and to confuse the Germans about British intentions. A mist on the morning of 8 August assisted surprise. After a brief bombardment, the long lines of tanks and infantry swept forward. The joint attack mostly unfolded as intended. The Australians in the centre reached their first objective at 7 a.m. and their second at 10.30 a.m. The Canadians on the left were alongside them at 11 a.m. Just over 2 hours later the main fighting was finished, the Australians having gained almost all of their objectives while the Canadians had advanced 7 miles. While the later stages of the battle did not yield as much as its beginning promised it was a distinct success, mainly because of good Corps command, rather than Army command.

Ludendorff writes in his memoirs, '8 August was the black day of the German army, the worst day I ever went through. We had to resign ourselves now to a continuation of the enemy's offensive. Their success had been too easy. Their wireless was jubilant, announcing with truth that the morale of the German army was no longer what it had been.'

As always, British casualties were heavy – 189,000 men between 8 August and 26 September. 'Men' is too general a term, since 50 per cent of the British casualties were hastily trained youths of 18 and 19, dredged from the bottom of the manpower barrel.

The American Commander-in-Chief, General John Pershing, was increasingly impatient for a major role in the fighting. In March there had been only 300,000 American troops in France but they were arriving at the rate of 300,000 a month, and Pershing was confident that his fresh, strong young men were ready for serious combat. Also, he wanted the US forces to be a separate army and not amalgamated with Allied units.

With the German tide stemmed, Pershing again pressed his demands. After much wrangling and many insults, the French and British agreed to allow the Americans to have a sure victory. A suitable target was found – the St Mihiel Salient, a German bulge in the French lines. On 12 September the American First Army commenced a barrage with 4,000 guns and then sent in 20 divisions – the equivalent of 40 British divisions – in a pincer attack against eight weary and undermanned German divisions. Holger Harwig[8] says, 'Since the enemy was actually in the process of evacuating the salient it is not too far off the mark to state that the Americans "relieved the Germans".'

Lloyd George, the CIGS, Wilson, Winston Churchill and Marshal Foch thought the final offensive should come in 1919. Haig was confident that the great breakthrough should be made in autumn 1918. Lloyd George's caution and his fears were understandable. With Haig's Somme and Third Ypres disasters in his mind, and conscious of the damage done to the British and Empire armies by the 1918 German offensives, the Prime Minister had an almost pathological fear that Haig would waste his reserves in a premature attack. Even Haig's strongest supporter, Lord Milner – who had become Secretary of State for War on 19 April – was worried and told him, later in September, that if he lost his army there were, finally, no more men available to replace it. Haig pacified Milner and convinced Foch that the Germans would break.

The attack opened on 27 September. In the north, the Belgians advanced 8 miles and recaptured Passchendaele but the advance was yet again held up by mud. In the south the French made an initial advance and were blocked by German resistance.

In the Meuse–Argonne sector, the final French–American

offensive was based on the assumption that the Ardennes forest was impenetrable. The French–American command planned to squeeze the Germans against this supposedly natural barrier while sealing off all avenues of retreat. The forest was not impenetrable, which the French, if not the Americans, should have known. Roads and railways ran through the forest and the Germans used them steadily. In addition, the German High Command had studied Petain's successful methods of elastic defence and copied them.

Luring the Americans on, they caused heavy casualties and on 26 September the great American assault came to grief against the Hindenburg Line. Recriminations erupted on all sides. The French generals complained that the Americans had learnt nothing about modern trench warfare. The French premier, Georges Clemenceau, went over Pershing's head to appeal to President Wilson for greater American vigour at the front. For his part, Pershing blamed the stalled offensive on his commanders and replaced them en masse.

The British armies, on 29 September, began an advance which broke through the southern part of the Hindenburg Line and 4 days later they were in open country behind the last German defences. The Australians, who had spearheaded this attack, were withdrawn on 3 October – for good, as it turned out. This was a fine feat of arms but it could not be exploited. There were not enough men to capture the railways and adequate supplies could not be brought up. As always, the German machine-gunners fought stubborn rearguard actions.

In October the Americans, despite the help of 3,000 guns and 189 tanks, again failed to penetrate the German's elastic defence. Eventually and inevitably, American weight proved to be decisive. From 1 November Pershing's forces began to advance rapidly along both sides of the Meuse river and were threatening from the south the last German line of retreat. On 4 November the British broke through the enemy lines of defence between the Schelde and the Sambre, capturing 20,000 prisoners and 450 guns.

The Armistice was signed a week later.

Haig's apologists claim that the victories of summer 1918 prove his qualities of leadership. This is not so. On the contrary, he had taken some steps which might have resulted in defeat, rather than victory. For instance, in February GHQ informed Colonel Fuller that the Commander-in-Chief proposed to reduce the Tank Corps by one third and that the vehicles would be used as strongpoints behind the British front lines. If, by this time, Haig was in any doubt about the essential role of tanks he could not have been planning for victory.

In August, during the Battle of Amiens, tanks working with infantry achieved a dramatic breakthrough south of the Somme river, but GHQ then pointlessly and wastefully ordered in the 3rd Cavalry Division. The horsemen did what the cavalry generals, especially Haig, had long wanted them to do – they galloped dashingly into action. Indeed, they charged ahead of their tanks and infantry and ran into German machine-gun fire, as was only to be expected. They were rescued by British tanks and Australian infantry. In clinging so long to the concept of cavalry exploitation Haig was apparently unaware, or heedless of, the changing face of warfare in 1918.

Haig has been praised for having predicted that the war would end in 1918. Such a prediction required no genius. All the necessary factors for success now applied, most importantly the readiness of a vast American army to take the field, and the devastation to the German economy by the Royal Navy's blockade.

It can only be admitted in Haig's favour that, in 1918, he was one of the first to see that a breakthrough was under way; also, he urged forward those generals, including Foch, who were inclined to stop. The German army of summer 1918 was weaker and more extended than it had been at any time and Haig's defenders claim that this was the result of his planning and leadership. More accurately, it was *despite* his leadership. If the relative German weakness really was the result of Haig's attack-and-attack-again policy then he had brought it about at a grossly unacceptable cost in British and Empire lives.

Haig had not smashed the German army and he admitted as

much when he urged that the Germans be offered moderate armistice terms. 'Germany is not broken in the military sense,' he reported. 'During the last weeks its armies have withdrawn fighting very bravely and in excellent order.'

NOTES

1. Holger H. Herwig and Neil M. Hayman, *Biographical Dictionary of World War I*. Greenwood Press, Connecticut, 1982.
2. David Woodward, *Lloyd George and the Generals*, Delaware, 1983.
3. Tim Travers, *The Killing Ground*, op. cit.
4. Paul Fussell, *The Great War and Modern Memory*, Oxford University Press, 1975. Fussell's book is a study of some of the literary means by which the war has been 'remembered, conventionalized and mythologized'.
5. Captain J.C. Dunn, *The War the Infantry Knew*, Jane's Publishing, 1987.
6. Lloyd George, *My War Memoirs*, op. cit.
7. Sir John Monash, *The Australian Victories in France in 1918*, Hutchinson, 1920.
8. Herwig, op. cit.

12

'MASTER of the FIELD'

'A Confession of Impotency'

SIR LLEWELLYN WOODWARD,
GREAT BRITAIN AND THE WAR OF 1914–1918

One historian of the Great War, Charles Fair,[1] says, 'It is hard for a connoisseur of bad generalship surveying the grey wastes of World War I, to single out any one commander as especially awful. There were dozens of them on both sides.'

A modern Briton may take 'both sides' to mean Britain and Germany. In fact, there were 'bad' generals in the armies of Austria, Serbia, Italy, France, Russia and the United States, as well as in those of Britain and Germany. A lot of the incompetent generals were 'bad' in a passive sense; that is, they allowed their opponents to dictate the course of warfare. The bunglers among the British and French were actively and wilfully bad; they threw lives away almost as if they had a mission to reduce the national population. Their bungling was callous and culpable and led to butchery.

That the British *and* French generals should both act in this way has a link. Throughout the war the British seemed to think that the French were masters of warfare, and they went on holding that belief long after the French generals had proved the notion wrong. Foch began the war with the maxim 'Attaque! Attaque! Attaque'. This maxim also links the French and British. For the greater part of the war the British generals also attacked,

attacked and attacked, without tactical subtlety or refinement.

For the three thousand years of recorded warfare surprise has been proved to be the key to victory. The annals of military history up to 1914 were full of classic instances of surprise as the basis for success. Haig was militarily educated; he must have known about this fundamental of war, yet he did not attempt to use it in his major campaigns and did not encourage his subordinate commanders to do so. For him, attrition was the great truth.

The traditional defence of Haig – and of French before him – is based on the assumption that a long, hard grind was the only way to victory. This may be the wrong defence for both men. A better plea in mitigation could be based on 'diminished responsibility' resulting from dull minds. It could be shown that French and Haig personified much of what was wrong with the entire British Army. Disciplined to the point of stupor, austere and aloof, these two commanders-in-chief discouraged criticism – even resented it – and avoided liberal discussion.

Shortly after the war Haig was invited to London to advise the Committee of Imperial Defence on certain technical matters. Before leaving for home he gave a dinner party attended by General Hubert Gough, Brigadier-General James Edmonds and Maurice Hankey, the Cabinet Secretary. Hankey asked Haig whether he felt that his Flanders' decisons of 1917 were the right ones. Haig replied 'without any note of hesitation' that he had no doubt about this. He described Flanders as simply a continuation of the Battle of the Somme and an essential factor in wearing down German resistance. On the whole, he told Hankey, it was less costly in casualties to attack than to defend. It is difficult to understand how he could still say this, when the true casualty figures for his battles were already known.

The Germans, Haig went on, were so exhausted by the 'remorseless hammering' he had given them in 1916 and 1917 that their efforts in their own great spring offensive of 1918 had finished them. This had enabled the Allies, reinforced by American troops, to 'reap the harvest sown on the Somme and in Flanders'. When making notes about the conversation, Hankey observed that Haig's mind was 'completely free from anything in the nature of self-reproach.'[2]

It is suggested that there has been a conspiracy to protect Haig's reputation, a conspiracy of senior army officers mostly. Such a conspiracy is believable. Haig's blunders were so great and his casualties so vast that they reflect on the Army's top leadership as a whole. Perhaps these leaders therefore felt compelled to defend Haig for their own sake. If they had criticised his leadership they would leave themselves open to the question, 'Why didn't *you* do something about it?' Also it was difficult for some officers to accept that such an appalling waste of life could be the result of a few military leaders' faults. To accept this would have been tantamount to admitting complicity in the slaughter. Instinctively, then, they closed ranks to form a lager in which Haig could find protection.

The most defensive of all Haig's former staff were Dewar and Boraston, in their two volumes *Sir Douglas Haig's Command 1915–1918*:[3]

> In his final despatch, the Commander-in-Chief, under the heading of 'A Single Great Britain', shows in a few passages how his own series of victories between the Battle of Amiens, August 8–13, 1918 and the Battle of the Sambre, November 1–11, 1918, were made possible and were gradually led up to by the wearing-down campaign of the preceding years. Those are illuminating passages! True, we can reach his conclusions by a careful independent study of the Despatches generally. They are clear logical deductions which a reader with common sense may reach for himself unaided. But it is fortifying for those among us who never wavered in the conviction that costly offensives in 1916 and 1917 were necessary before the immense military power of Germany could be brought down in 1918 to have the truth set forth in perfectly simple terms through a master-mind in war; through the strategist who wrought the weapon and dealt the stroke.

Here, after the war, we have two of Haig's staff justifying his strategy and tactics. They could do nothing else since they were part of Haig's retinue during the war, when they had endorsed his strategy and tactics. Anticipating certain criticisms, Dewar and Boraston beat the critics to the punch. 'But, it may be objected, the costly offensives of 1916 and 1917 did not always work out according to plan: the hoped-for breakthrough, for instance, to the first Battle of the Somme was not effective. It would have been a miracle had they always worked out according to plan. No reasoned defence of British or French strategy would make such an idiotic claim as that.'

Despite the Dewar–Boraston disclaimer, Haig and his Army commanders *expected* the plan to work out according to plan. Why otherwise would Rawlinson have said that all that was necessary on 1 July was for the troops to stroll over and take the German trenches after the British guns had finished with them? The Dewar–Boraston phraseology is that of men staging a last-ditch verbal defence of their chief and, indirectly, of themselves. 'There is only one witness to genius whose evidence is unimpeachable, the witness Time,' say Dewar and Boraston. 'The others may not be of more weight in war than in art or in letters. Time, the supreme arbiter, will disclose whether or not "genius" contrived that magnificent British plan of 8 August–11 November, 1918. We may leave it at that.'

On 21 March 1919 Haig published his Final Despatch. In effect, it is a summary together with a justification for his strategy and tactics and a rationalisation about casualties. His sub-headings are listed as: *A Single Great Battle, The Length of the War, The Extent of Our Casualties, Why We Attacked Whenever Possible, The End of the War.*

Certain statements in the Final Despatch need emphasis and provoke comment:

A Single Great Battle

'To direct attention to any single phase of that stupendous and incessant struggle and seek in it the explanation of our success, to the exclusion or neglect of other phases possibly less striking in their immediate or obvious consequences, it is my opinion to risk the formation of unsound doctrines regarding the character and requirements of modern war.'

Haig attempts here to block analysis of the Somme offensive in 1916 and other abortive and bloody pushes.

'If the whole operations of the present war are regarded in

correct perspective, the victories of the summer and autumn of 1918 will be seen to be directly dependent upon the two years of stubborn fighting that preceded them.'

The 'correct perspective' is, of course, Haig's perspective. This is another attempt to rationalise the disasters of 1916–18 and disguise the reality of slaughter by calling them 'stubborn fighting'.

The Length of the War

'The huge numbers of men engaged on either side, whereby a continuous battle front was rapidly established from Switzerland to the sea, outflanking was made impossible and manoeuvre very difficult, necessitating the delivery of frontal attacks. This factor, combined with the strength of the defensive under modern conditions, rendered a protracted wearing-out battle unavoidable [and] a long struggle for supremacy inevitable.'

Anticipating further criticisms of his tactics and his losses, Haig indulges in pre-emptive rationalisation.

The Extent of our Casualties

'Given the military situation existing in August 1914, our total losses in the war have been no larger than were to be expected. Neither do they compare unfavourably with those of any other of the belligerent nations. The total British casualties in all theatres of war – killed, wounded and prisoners, including native troops – are approximately three millions. Of this total 2,568,834 were incurred on the Western Front.'

An admission by Haig that he expected massive casualties. In any case, he offers the comforting reflection that we lost no more men than the other armies.

Why We Attacked Whenever Possible

'A defensive policy involves the loss of the initiative, with all the consequent disadvantages to the defender. The enemy is able to choose at his own convenience the time and place of his attacks.'

After trench lines were established in 1915 the Germans, as defenders, suffered few disadvantages. Their defences were infinitely better than those of the British and French. The enemy – in this case, the British – certainly chose the time and place of attacks and paid a terrible price for this privilege. The German defenders also chose the time and place for their counter-attacks, two of which came dangerously close to smashing the Allied lines.

The End of the War

'It is in the great battles of 1916 and 1917 that we have to seek for the secret of our victory in 1918.'

It is difficult to read this statement without a feeling of outrage. For the British and French, the battles of 1916 and 1917 were failures. Haig, then, is saying that failure was the 'secret' of success. Moreover, his use of the word secret would appear to indicate that he deliberately failed so as to bring about eventual success. Since he cannot possibly mean this – it is nonsense – the statement can only be a rationalisation, though a perverted one. In effect, Haig tries to justify the 1916 and 1917 failures by the achievement of final victory.

Haig's most ardent defender and apologist was Major-General Sir John Davidson, Director of Operations in France 1916–18:[4]

I cannot help referring to Haig's determination, moral courage, military knowledge, foresight and long sight and even second sight, his unswerving loyalty and imperturbility throughout adversity and good fortune alike, his equable relations with his Allies who were failing him but were, at the same time, receiving his unfailing help and sympathy throughout their difficulties. He fulfilled his task with tenacity, consummate skill and complete success. He met every crisis with careful forethought, calculated prevision and sound judgment. He kept the respect and confidence of the men who fought under him and he preserved their splendid morale.

This is syncophancy to the point of absurdity.

For the title of his book Davidson chose *Haig – Master of the Field*. This was a quotation from a comment by Ludendorff[5] that at the end of the war Haig 'and he alone, stood master of the field'. Ever since then Haig's supporters have assumed, or pretended, that this is an unqualified compliment. But Luden-dorff did not mean that Haig had won the field by strategic and tactical brilliance and sheer leadership.

He meant that of all the senior commanders who were in place early in the war only Haig remained at the end. For France, Joffre, Petain and Nivelle had come and gone; for Germany, Moltke, Falkenhayn and Bülow no longer held pre-eminent positions; for Russia, Brusilov and Ivanov had gone, as had Cadorna, for Italy. For Britain, French had been replaced by Haig himself. Even Ludendorff did not see out the war as Germany's generalissimo; he resigned on 29 October 1918. Foch, French military commander at the end of the war, had not served as long as Haig at the top. By stubborn persistence and royal patronage, Haig had held onto the British command so that he was the leader when the war ended. As the senior surviving general, of course he 'stood master of the field'. Ludendorff's words were meant to be figurative. They could be nothing else, since Foch, as the Allied supremo, was military master of the field at the time of the armistice.

Some praise for Haig is extravagant and ridiculous. General James Marshall-Cornwall,[6] likens him to the American Civil War General Ulysses Grant. He recalls that a year after General Lee, leader of the Confederate army, surrendered at Appomattox, Grant said to a British visitor: 'My object in war was to exhaust Lee's army. I was obliged to sacrifice men to do it. I have been called a butcher. Well, I never spared men's lives to gain an object, but then I gained it, and I knew it was the only way.'

Commenting on this, Marshall-Cornwall says: 'It was the only way in 1861–1865, and it was the only way in 1914–1918. There was no short and bloodless cut to victory. Lloyd George's alternative strategy of "knocking away German's props" was logistically impracticable and would have led to military disaster. Douglas Haig and Ulysses Grant may perhaps share the honours as "four-star generals" in the galaxy of Great Captains.'

Apart from other considerations, General Grant was not a remote figure, whereas Haig was a God-like creature. Even when he appeared at conferences or at an Army HQ, or anywhere else, he was distant in manner and his numerous staff 'protected' him from practically everyone. It took even a determined Army commander to break through the staff cordon.

Colonel Rowland Feilding,[7] one of the war's most successful regimental commanders, was once asked, when on leave, what the men thought of Haig. Feilding was both startled and amused by the question because he knew that the men had no thoughts about Haig. In a letter to his wife, Feilding commented on his friend's naive question. 'The *men*, and by a very intelligent man, too. It was during one of the bad times. He asked me this question and added: "If by now, they don't look on him as a demi-god, it proves that he is not the right person and ought to go."'

'You might as well ask what the private soldier thinks of God. He knows about the same amount of each. Though I have been in every army in France even I have never seen the Commander-in-Chief. I have only seen my Army Commander on four occasions in over three years – Plumer twice and Birdwood twice.'

Since 1918 many people – academics, miltiary historians, soldiers of all ranks, official correspondents, statesmen – have judged Haig, and through him, other British generals. Some of the criticisms merely detail his failings, others are more damning. This is a selection of them.

Paul Fussell[8]

One doesn't want to be too hard on Haig, who doubtless did all he could and who has been well calumniated already. But it must be said that it now appears that one thing the war was testing was the usefulness of the earnest Scottish character in a situation demanding the military equivalent of wit and invention. Haig had none. He was stubborn, self-righteous, inflexible, intolerant – especially of the French – and quite humourless. Bullheaded as he was, he was the perfect commander for an enterprise committed to endless abortive assaults.

Duff Cooper[9]

Haig was as good a general as it is possible for a man without genius to become.

Cooper was actually *praising* Haig.

Brigadier-General E.L. Spears[10]

Douglas Haig was well versed in his profession, with a clear vision over a limited field, but he suffered from the handicap inherent in men who know what they want and see their goal, but are conscious that they lack the gift of persuasion. He expressed himself clearly and forcibly on paper. A hesitant speech, ending in a sentence reinforced by a forward movement of the jaw giving the impression that obstinacy rather than reason dictated his decisions, stood him in poor stead when dealing with Ministers.

Sir Llewellyn Woodward[11]

Haig reached opinions slowly and held to them. He made up his mind in 1915 that the war could be won on the Western Front, and only on the Western Front. He acted on this view, and, at the last, he was right, though it is open to argument not only that victory could have been won sooner elsewhere but that Haig's method of winning it was clumsy, tragically expensive of life and based for too long on a misreading of the facts.

Woodward says of cavalry officers generally:

The average of intelligence among British cavalry officers, notwithstanding their personal courage, was notoriously lower than that of the engineer and artillery officers.

Woodward again:

The policy of attrition or in plain English, killing Germans until the German army was worn down and exhausted, was not only wasteful and, intellectually, a confession of impotency; it was also extremely dangerous.

Brigadier-General Sir James Edmonds[12]

I have to write of Haig with my tongue in my cheek. One can't tell the truth. He really was above the – or rather, below the average in stupidity.

Major-General Sir Ernest Swinton[13]

Haig was steeped in tradition and very industrious. His reception of a new idea like tanks was beneath contempt. French was a stupid ill-educated man. Haig was a stupid man but better educated.

Barrie Pitt[14]

Haig remained for too long unaware of the value to his country of the men entrusted to his care.

If failure of policy caused the war, failure on the part of the military leaders was responsible for its cost. The Allied generals especially seemed to measure the success of their own projects in terms of the size of their own casualty figures.

Lloyd George[15]

He was brilliant to the top of his boots. [Actually, Lloyd George and a friend were looking at a portrait of Haig in uniform, including his famous shiny boots. With his finger, Lloyd George drew a line across the top of the boots and said, 'He was brilliant up to there.']

Dr C.E.W. Bean[16]

In several of his massively detailed and highly acclaimed Australian official histories, Bean refers to Haig and gives his assessment of the Commander-in-Chief. As was his way, Bean strove to be fair.

With his many qualities of greatness, his judgment of men was far from infallible, and, once his confidence had been gained, his trust was blind, not to say obstinate. At dinner, an old friend asked Haig whether he was aware of the opinions about Gough that were widespread in the army. Haig replied curtly that he wished to hear nothing on the subject.

Attrition, as Haig seems to have conceived it, was a bludgeoning process, repellent to many agile minds, but by ingenuity it could be made terribly effective.

Haig rarely exhibited a spark of brilliance.

Haig never gave up hoping that the initial surprise and confusion might be prolonged by cavalry carrying out its traditional role, but telephone, motor vehicle and machine-gun had changed all that. Cavalry was now too slow and vulnerable to fulfil its old role, at least on the highly organised Western Front. On August 8, near Harbonniéres, Somme, a dozen armoured cars achieved more than an entire cavalry brigade.

Except for a first-rate mind – which Haig lacked – training in military history and tradition could actually confuse judgment in such matters. It is conceivable that, had Haig grasped earlier the possibilities of the tank, he might have forestalled history by securing an effective 'mounted arm' at half the trouble and cost with which the British cavalry was maintained, uselessly, on the Western Front.

Arthur Behrand[17]
I was shocked, many years later, to learn of Haig's pettiness, obstinacy and obtuseness. Surely he was the first British military leader to hang himself by his own diaries and letters.

Sir Basil Liddell Hart[18]
Haig had an impregnable capacity for holding even the most willing at a distance . . . inflexibly consistent, and persistent . . . the opening of the mouth automatically cut out the action of the brain.

Field Marshal Lord Montgomery[19]
Haig was unimaginative. Maybe he was competent according to his lights, but these were dim. Confidence of divine approval appeared to satisfy him. Nothing can excuse the casualties of the Somme and Passchendaele. Furthermore, he intrigued against his commander-in-chief [Lloyd George] and his political masters, which in my view is unforgiveable, even though he was himself intrigued against.

Paul Kennedy[20]
Leadership was changing but this does not seem as if it were due to a rethinking at GHQ where Haig's performance until the bitter end of the Passchendaele campaign showed the same incomprehension of the realities of frontline conflict as before.

Brian Gardner[21]
Haig's defenders have always been wrong. Mostly military men, some of them ex-staff officers, they have appeared at times

something like an unorganised conspiracy to protect his reputation. They realise that the present decade is a vital one in the final assessment of the man, that the present judgment is likely to be the one handed down in history.

For several reasons, it is surprising that the British army, of all armies, was not the most advanced and eager in new tactical ideas. For instance, the British army had an ongoing history of hundreds of small wars, in all of which mobility was emphasised. By late 1917, if not before, numerous innovative and bright officers were advocating greater sophistication in artillery support and urging flexible, small-unit attacks. The British, because of Churchill, Fuller, Swinton and others, were furthest ahead in tank development. This was the most revolutionary answer to the problem of mobile firepower. On top of all this, the British complained much more loudly about the butchery in the trenches than did any other belligerent nation. This should have done much to bring about tactical changes.

The dull, inflexible Haig and the other generally dull and unimaginative senior officers stood firmly in the way of real change. Just as seriously, the many lessons learnt at the front either did not get back to the various senior Staffs or were not acted upon. To use a much more modern term, there was no adequate feedback.

In contrast, the German army had an efficient feedback system. The German High Command has been criticised as hidebound and rigid but it was nothing of the sort. The German General Staff was ready to listen to ideas from the ranks. New ideas were transformed into new methods, tactics and organisation. Among the most effective ideas was the withdrawal to a shorter stronger line in the latter stages of the 1916 Somme battles and the use of defensive posts rather than trench lines during Third Ypres, 1917.

It is not a matter of hindsight to say that during the 1914–18 war whichever army went forward in the traditional way – with soldiers spread in rows across the battlefield – it at once put itself under a great disadvantage because it was bound to suffer heavy casualties and was risking defeat. Expressed another way, one side began to lose its advantage as soon as it began an offensive against the other, because the defenders were not exposed. That this disadvantage for the attackers was understood by the generals of the time can be proved: the attackers generally felt that they needed a numerical superiority of three to one. This superiority was to compensate for the heavy casualties that they anticipated. It was the H.C.I. fixation at work.

There was a concommitant disadvantage in developing the three to one or higher ration. It brought numerous other problems into play, such as supply and transport and evacuation of the wounded.

Many senior British generals, including most of those whose conduct is described in this book, were victims of a strange type of intellectual paralysis – the paralysis of the push. Unhappily, this mental paralysis goaded them into powerful physical action, which they planned in three phases. First the artillery blazed away for days against the enemy trenches; the heavily laden infantry went over the top towards those trenches; the cavalry chafed at the bit as they waited to charge through the breach. No breach occurred for years but the masses of cavalry kept on waiting. They were a standing indictment of the paralysed minds which kept them there.

The paralysis of the push appeared to be incurable. Hunter-Weston demonstrated it at Cape Helles, Gallipoli, and was afflicted by it throughout the war on the Western Front. Gough, Haking and Rawlinson, all suffered from it, and Haig most chronically of all. Allenby shared it while in France but recovered in Palestine.

Physically and mentally distanced from the realities of the battlefields, Haig and his GHQ did little more than call for more men and guns. In this GHQ was backed by the CIGS Robertson until his removal only in 1918. At the same time there went out from Haig and GHQ the traditional clarion call for Corps and Divisional generals to inspire their men to ever great effort and gallantry.

The generals' ever increasing hunger for guns can be shown by simple statistics. The preliminary bombardment of the battle of Hooge (Ypres Salient) in May 1915 required 18,000 shells; for First Somme, from 24 June to 1 July, 2,000,000 and for Third Ypres, 16–31 July 1917, 4,300,000 shells.

Let it be said that the troops were not at fault. They kept faith with their generals, bunglers or not, even if the converse did not apply. French's professionals in 1914 and early 1915 were superb soldiers. Those men who went to Gallipoli in April 1915, the first Australian and New Zealand volunteers and British regulars, fought with amazing spirit and endurance. Then the Yeomanry regiments, at Suvla Bay from August onwards, fought as best they could under a wholly useless commander, Stopford, and mediocre divisional generals. Despite all the initial handicaps which Hamilton faced he could have done better with such soldiers in his ranks.

Townshend's troops in Mesopotamia gave him their loyalty, their strength and finally their liberty and lives. He betrayed them. In France, from the time that Kitchener's New Armies first arrived they impressed observers with their spirit and enthusiasm. The young officers were magnificent material. Shocked and bewildered, the New Armies marched into massacre on the Somme.

From the latter half of 1916 men from Britain and its empire reached the battle lines in their tens of thousands. In some ways the boys and the middle-aged men who were sent to the slaughter after March 1918 were very special, the older men in particular. They were unfit and knew the risks but duty took them forward.

To draw distinctions between the military prowess of the Australians, Canadians and New Zealanders – collectively the 'Colonials', – and the English, Scots, Welsh and Irish, is invidious and unnecessary. And the Gurkhas and Indians were no less than the others. All reflected their racial and social background, which made them 'different' one from the other. The records show that certain divisions did not perform well at certain times. This is much more a reflection on their senior leadership than on the men.

The Australians have always felt that they were overused in

comparison with what they called 'Imperial troops' – those from the British Isles. There is no proof of this, as C.E.W. Bean conceded. When it came to bungling, and therefore butchery, the British generals who form the core of this book were impartial. They fed divisions into the meat grinder without favouritism.

That senior military leaders were aware of the failures is evident from their attempts to cover up mistakes made during the war. This is evidence of the 'unorganised conspiracy' to which Gardner refers. They tampered with the military record – as in army, corps and GHQ diaries, and they tried to influence what was written in the *Official History*. They were fortunate in having the support of the official historian himself, Brigadier-General Edmonds.

Edmonds had been one of Haig's close friends at Staff College, where Haig became Edmonds' protector. After the war Edmonds repaid Haig by preserving his reputation while writing the *Official History*. This is particularly noticeable in his volume on Passchendaele.

Tim Travers,[22] who has studied Edmonds' methods, says that he toned down offending passages or placed 'awkward evidence' in footnotes or simply confined the text to facts. 'Edmonds tended increasingly to defend Haig and the GHQ point of view, and sometimes altered the text to support Haig and GHQ,' Travers says. 'The general conclusion must be that Edmonds often altered passages to suit the criticism of senior commanders, and certainly sought to diminish the worst errors.'

We now know that not all of Haig's diary was written up at the time and that some important material was inserted later, and some was deleted, by himself or others. Lady Haig stated in a letter that she had omitted various passages and had also altered some words in line with a proposal to do so by her husband.

The conspiracy to protect Haig's reputation was evident in an editorial in *The Army Quarterly* of April 1928, following Haig's death earlier that year. One passage in the long eulogy attracts the attention of anybody reading it critically.

'His toughness of fibre, his determination to do the right thing by his troops regardless of the cost to himself. . . .'

What *right thing* had he done for his troops? There is little evidence that he did anything for his troops. He could not even, by his own admission, bear to visit the wounded in hospital. Over and over again he had asked the impossible of his troops. And at what *cost to himself*? He suffered in no way.

If we accept, with Paul Kennedy and others, that Haig and others lacked comprehension we are, in effect, excusing them their blunders. When a man cannot see that a problem exists he can hardly be expected to seek a remedy for it. No British general of World War I could have failed to realise that serious problems existed. The war was not being won and casualties were running into hundreds of thousands dead and millions wounded. These problems could not have escaped anybody's comprehension.

Haig and other British generals must be indicted not for incomprehension but for wilful blunders and wicked butchery. However stupid they might have been, however much they were the product of a system which obstructed enterprise, they knew what they were doing. There can never be forgiveness.

In 1926 Haig commented in a book review: 'I believe that the value of the horse and the opportunity of the horse in the future are likely to be as great as ever. Aeroplanes and tanks are only accessories to the men and the horse, and I feel sure that as time goes on you will find just as much use for the horse – the well-bred horse – as you have ever done in the past.'

The well-bred horse, to be sure! After his 4 years on the Western Front Haig had learnt absolutely nothing.

In a famous utterance, Georges Clemenceau said that modern war was 'too important to be left to the generals'. But between 1914 and 1918 it *had been* left to the generals and therein lies the enduring tragedy.

NOTES

1. Charles Fair, *From the Jaws of Victory*, London, 1930.
2. Lord Hankey, *The Supreme Command 1914–18*, op. cit.

3. G.A.B. Dewar and Lieut.-Colonel J.H. Boraston, op. cit.
4. Sir John Davidson, *Haig – Master of the Field*, Peter Nevill, London, 1953.
5. General Erich Ludendorff, *My War Memoirés*, London, 1926.
6. General Sir James Marshall-Cornwall, *Haig As a Military Commander*, Batsford, London, 1973.
7. Colonel Rowland Feilding, *War Letters to a Wife*, London, 1929.
8. Paul Fussell, *The Great War and Modern Memory*, op. cit.
9. Duff Cooper, *Haig*, Faber & Faber, London, 1936.
10. Major-General E.L. Spears, *Liaison 1914*, op. cit.
11. Sir Llewellyn Woodward, *Great Britain and the war of 1914–1918*, op. cit.
12. Brigadier-General James Edmonds, the Official Historian, made this comment in a conversation with Liddell Hart.
13. Major-General Ernest Swinton, *Eyewitness, 1932*. Swinton was one of the most important tank pioneers, perhaps the most important.
14. Barrie Pitt, *1918 The Last Act*, op. cit.
15. David Lloyd-George, *War Memoirs*, op. cit.
16. C.E.W. Bean, The Australian Official War Correspondent and Official Historian, op. cit.
17. Arthur Behrand, *As From Kemmel Hill*, op. cit.
18. Sir Basil Liddell-Hart, *History of the First World War*, op. cit.
19. Field Marshal Lord Montgomery, *A History of Warfare*, Collins, London, 1968. Montgomery and I discussed, several times during the 1960s, leadership in general and that of 1914–18 in particular. He had served as a young officer in the war and was seriously wounded. He said that his own observations and experiences profoundly influenced his attitude to casualties when he was a Commander-in-Chief during the Second World War.
20. Paul Kennedy of Yale University, in an essay, 'Britain in the First World War', published in *Military Effectiveness: The First World War*, Allen & Unwin, London, 1980.
21. Brian Gardner, *The Big Push*, Cassell, London, 1961.
22. Tim Travers, *The Killing Ground*, op. cit.

13

WHO WON?

What Else?

Two points remain to be dealt with, if only briefly. Who won the war? What else could British (and French) generals have done to achieve an earlier and less costly victory?

1. It can be stated flatly that neither the British army nor the French army, nor both of them together, won the war, for the German army was not defeated and did not collapse. The Americans did not win the war, though their impressive and rapidly increasing strength convinced the Germans that they could no longer hold out. The Royal Air Force, which by mid-1918 was a potent bombing force, did not win the war. While the war had not been decided in the air, the race for supremacy quickly produced remarkable developments.

It was the Royal Navy, unseen by Europe as a whole, which played the most decisive part in winning the war. In February 1916, a Ministry of Blockade was set up and went a long way beyond merely trying to prevent the shipment of contraband cargoes, such as war materials. Many successful attempts were made to stop Europeans from selling surplus products to Germany, such as fish from the North Sea. Rubber and oil were not reaching the Germans. The effect of many pressures, by the end of 1916, has been called 'the most devastating, offensive use of sea power devised in war'. Food riots took place in Germany and the 'turnip winter' of 1916–17 imposed severe hardship on the German populace.

The German U-boat campaign of sinking merchant ships which were supplying Britain was damaging but not crippling. The

---

British blockade bit harder into Germany's economy than the submarine campaign damaged that of Britain. In the end, the convoy system adopted by British reduced the U-boat threat.

During the German breakthroughs of March and April 1918 the ill-fed German troops were astounded by the amount and variety of food they captured in Allied dumps. The impetus of their drive slackened while the hungry troops gorged themselves. The letters which they sent home about the food available to the British troops disheartened their families, who were living on meagre rations.

In the final analysis, the war was won by the Germans' awareness that American military might seemed to be inexhaustible and their despair caused by the blockade.

2.   It is not true that attrition – that is reciprocal slaughter – was the 'only way' to win the war. Various options, all within the capabilities of the time, were available.

French and then Haig could have done *less*. Having found out that old-fashioned frontal assaults did not work it was not necessary to continue to make them. The Germans had invaded Belgium and France and they had been stopped along the Western Front. If they wanted to capture Paris and the Channel ports it was up to the German leadership to break through. The British High Command could have 'invited' the Germans to attack, on ground of Allied choosing, and then inflicted heavy casualties.   It was always a mistake for the British to get bogged in the foul mire of Flanders. Instead, by holding in strength the 'seven mountains of Flanders' [hills, actually] they should have allowed the Germans to move into the lowlands where they could have been made to endure the level of casualties and misery which the British suffered by holding the lowlands. From the seven mountains every German position would have been well within artillery range and from some of them observation was excellent. The British did, in fact, hold the 'seven mountains' until the German breakthrough of April 1918 and there was no tactical reason for the High Command to crowd its own troops into the lowlands.

Flexible defence was always possible. The Germans used it,

notably during Third Ypres, and so did the French in 1917 and 1918. In effect, they held the front areas by scattered strongpoints rather than continuous trenches. These strongpoints held up an enemy assault for a certain length of time and inflicted casualties. Then the attackers, exhausted and depleted in numbers, ran against the main defence system and were stopped dead. In nearly every instance this pattern of aggressive defence succeeded at all levels from division to army.

The British (and French) could have used the 'von Hutier tactics' exploited by Ludendorff in the 1918 spring offensive. Basically, this meant a brief bombardment, use of machine-gun teams as probing scouts, bypassing of strongpoints and then massive infiltration.

Greater use of the Royal Navy as mobile heavy artillery could have helped. In 1917 Haig contemplated a great offensive up the Belgian coast in collaboration with the Royal Navy. This would outflank the German army and clear the Belgian channel ports from which U-boats were operating. After the success of the Messines offensive in July 1917 he came back to this idea, which seemed not only advantageous but desirable. In the first place, it offered the only possibility of opening up a flank and breaking the Western Front stalemate. Superior British sea power could guarantee supply of all that was needed in such a thrust. The coastal plan would exert such great pressure on the Germans that the French might have time to rebuild their battered and mutinous army.

Another factor influencing the go-for-the-coast plan was that the Russian Army was breaking up in the wake of the Revolution. This meant that the Germans could move large forces from the Eastern to the Western Front. The British attack had to be made before this happened. While these factors were being considered the Admiralty threw in another and more alarming factor. Unless the Channel ports held by the Germans were taken quickly and the U-boat bases destroyed the Allies were in danger of losing the war. Taken together, there were compelling reasons for the Allies to reach the coast.

Instead of trying to attack out of the Ypres Salient, Haig could have passed through the Belgian army which was holding the left or northern end of the Western Front. He would then have had the sea as his left flank, protected by the mighty battleships of the fleet. The idea was not tried.

A simple improvement of tactics would have been to attack without a preliminary bombardment – that is, in sudden surprise attacks. Surprise was conspicuously absent from British thinking until the middle of 1918.

Tanks could have been used more effectively – and would have been, had High Command taken the advice of the specialist tank officers. Cambrai showed what could be achieved. By building up a massive fleet of tanks and using them on carefully chosen ground – firm and not too sloping – a genuine breakthrough rather than a dent in the enemy line was possible from the middle of 1917. Using tanks during Third Ypres was pointless, as the Tank Corps men knew. But employing them in a major attack in firmer country at the same time as the Ypres battle may have produced a breaking strain on the German front.

Artillery and engineer generals were never adequately consulted. Had they been, then the result of certain offensives could have been different. The gunners did their best on the first day of the Somme but they were under the orders of senior generals steeped in cavalry tactics and timeworn infantry methods. The Royal Artillery had two clever innovative generals in Birch and Uniacke, but neither was even given enough responsibility.

All of the tactics mentioned here required experiment, enterprise, innovation and imagination, along the lines encouraged at Messines by Plumer and his Chief-of-Staff, Major-General Tim Harington. But these qualities were in short supply at GHQ and at most Army HQs. From the time he assumed command of the British Forces, Haig hung heavily over all the planning tables.

Field-Marshal Montgomery states; 'I would name Sir John Monash as the best general on the Western Front in Europe. He possessed real creative originality, and the war might well have been over sooner, and certainly with fewer casualties, had Haig been relieved of command and Monash appointed to command the British armies in his place.'

Montgomery wrote this in 1968 but he had always known that it was never remotely possible that Monash would be given command. He had not reached the Western Front until 1916, and until 1918 he was a mere lieut.-general, one of numerous officers of that rank. Above him were the five British Army commanders and others hoping for an Army Command. Monash was commanding only a Corps, and then only from the middle of 1918. Lloyd George had heard a lot about him but did not know him well. A 'colonial' and an amateur being given command of the British forces was inconceivable in 1918.

The Rewards

The senior generals were well rewarded for their labours. Field Marshals French and Haig were created Earls; Horne and Rawlinson Barons. Gough, Hunter-Weston, Hamilton, Kiggell, Haking, Harper, Stopford and Townshend all had knighthoods. Haig, already wealthy, received the thanks of parliament and a grant of £100,000. Some of the others were given £30,000. The ancestral home of the Haigs at Bemersyde, Scotland, was purchased by national subscription in 1921.

The generals of each of the Allied countries received decorations from every one of the others; this was a matter of custom and courtesy.

Apart from any decorations for bravery which they might have won, the ordinary soldiers were awarded the 1914–15 Star – if they qualified for this period – the War Medal and the Victory Medal. The great majority had only the latter two.

Next-of-kin of servicemen who gave their lives received a bronze memorial plaque which carried their name but no other details. Around the edge were the words, 'He died for freedom and honour.' With it came the dead serviceman's medals and a scroll of appreciation from the king, with the royal coat-of-arms. It read:

WHO WON?

He whom this scroll commemorates
was numbered among those who,
at the call of King and Country, left all
that was dear to them, endured hardness,
faced danger, and finally passed out of
the sight of men by the path of duty
and self-sacrifice, giving up their own
lives that others might live in freedom.
Let those who come after see to it
that his name be not forgotten.

(Name and regiment inscribed here)

Nearly one million of the plaques and scrolls were distributed. Just what proportion of the casualties was caused by bungling generals is impossible to estimate. During World War I the generals calculated to a nicety the number of men available 'for expenditure' in casualties. *Not one British general ever planned an operation on the basis of how many men could be brought through it alive.*

A great equestrian statue of Field Marshal Earl Haig stands in Whitehall opposite the Cenotaph, which commemorates the servicemen killed during the war. There could be no more appropriate location.

———————————— *14* ————————————

WHAT the SOLDIERS SAY

'Just One Long Degradation'

MAJOR SIDNEY BAKER, A LETTER FROM THE FRONT

It has been frequently said that the senior commanders whose strategy and tactics sent men into desperate battle had little or no conception of the appalling difficulties and dangers of warfare between 1914 and 1918. Two questions naturally follow from this assertion.

'How could they *not* have known?'

and

'If they did not know at the beginning surely they must have known after a few months' fighting in the battle of the Somme?'

Of course they should have known. Reports from their Intelligence staffs should have told them. The senior medical staff must have been aware of the ghastly nature of the wounds and casualties, and their official reports to Army HQs and to GHQ should have included reference to the horrors. Brigade commanders, who were sometimes not far behind the fighting lines, were in a position to see the battlefield conditions, and they heard frequently from their battalion commanders, who were further forward. Since the brigadiers were required to submit reports to

---

their divisional commander, it might be thought that such reports would emphasise the fearful nature of the battlefield if only to help explain the lack of progress.

Some commanders at battalion, brigade and divisional level did not like to talk or write about the conditions under which their men existed, fought and died because it was 'unsoldierly' to do so. After all, by British tradition, soldiering meant service and sacrifice without complaint. The Victorian attitude of 'Theirs not to reason why, theirs but to do and die,' was still strongly held. It is difficult to comprehend, in the late twentieth century, that when Tennyson wrote these immortal lines he was not being critical of British leadership. He was stating the obvious and the accepted and was virtually glorying in the death *and* glory charge. If soldiers were ordered to make an impossible suicidal charge, so be it. Having taken the Queen's Shilling, they had an obligation to die when called upon to do so, even when the call was patently absurd. Soldiers were not considered to have any right to apply reason to what they were doing.

During the war of 1914–18, some colonels, brigadier-generals and major-generals did tell the truth in their reports but left out the really unpleasant facts. Where it was necessary to give military information, they gave it. But this type of officer did not consider the difficulty of fighting in wet and wintry weather to be military information; nor was the oozing, greasy mud.

Nevertheless, many officers of the rank of major-general and below – that is, those officers more or less directly involved in combat – did write full and frank reports. Numerous Staff officers read these reports when they reached Corps HQ, Army HQ and GHQ. Some Staff officers would have gone fairly far forward on occasions – at least close enough to the action to see the burgeoning military cemeteries. Also, they could see, when they visited a dugout HQ, that the officers and men there were under great strain and were exhausted. Conscientious Staff officers actually reached the front line during battle, so that when they returned to their offices they really had something to talk about.

A few of the butchers and bunglers about whom I have written knew at first hand what their men endured. Hunter-Weston certainly knew at Helles, Gallipoli. The battlefield was small and once he came ashore from the comfort of his HQ on board a destroyer he could see the carnage for himself. At Kut, Townshend could not avoid seeing it and smelling it.

If we accept that the 'Great Captains' did not know what their infantry soldiers endured in the trenches we are, to an extent, excusing them their callousness; indeed, it is then only 'apparent callousness'. But they *did* know. The gunfire could clearly be heard even at Montreuil, where it sometimes kept the Staff awake at night. The officers here might never have seen the effects of a shell bursting amid a cluster of men, but they had all seen, on artillery ranges and in manoeuvres, the power of a mighty explosion. It did not take much imagination to picture the result of such a blast among men. Again, when rain fell at HQ it was almost certainly raining on the front line and sometimes the rain fell for days on end. HQ was generally in a chateau or hotel and water cascading down a windowpane was no more than an inconvenience to the man in a comfortable and heated building. Water steadily flooding a slimy trench and soaking into boots and clothing was a diabolical evil to the men who had no shelter from it. It might be thought that even the dullest senior commander would have a mental picture of the cold and wet, the strain and the hunger which his men were enduring.

French and Haig and their senior subordinates filtered the unpleasantness from their minds. Just as the windows kept the water from their persons, so they pulled down mental blinds to blot out the unpleasant, the ugly and the foul. When General Kiggell was caught out of doors towards the Front on just that one occasion in the rain and mud the blind sprang open and he was shocked.

But Kiggell had known all along what he was sending men into. All the generals knew but many chose not to acknowledge the truth. There is nothing in the memoirs of the 'Great Captains' to indicate that conversation in their comfortable messes ever turned to how 'the men' were faring. In the years when the Staff officers of 1914–18 were in their sixties and seventies I asked several of them if they had ever been shocked by the cruel realities of trench warfare. They could afford to be truthful in their advancing years and some said, in effect, 'It was ghastly, but what could be done about it?' Others said, 'Well, that was the kind of war we were in.'

Subconsciously, they were still chained to the Heavy Casualties Inevitable Fixation. Some of these men had convinced themselves that the heroism of so many men had somehow made the horrors less horrible, the blunders less serious, the scale of death and mutilation more acceptable. In doing so, they were deceiving their consciences.

For the duration of the war what the men were expected to endure as frontline soldiers was covered up. The generals used no phrase more revealing than 'difficult conditions'. The Church, in the persons of the senior chaplains at the war, probably knew the truth but did not attempt to bring it out. They, as members of the Establishment, did not want to criticise it. With few exceptions, the war correspondents did not write revealingly and critically about what they saw. They censored themselves more effectively than Army censors could have done.

The General Public knew that something was wrong. Widows and orphans were being created by the hundreds of thousands and limbless and otherwise mutilated men were returning to their home towns in droves. But the General Public bore their sufferings stoically, as was the custom. They did not know of anything else that might be done, even if, in this great war 'for civilisation', civilisation itself disappeared.

What sort of warfare killed so many men and so profoundly changed all those who survived it? The war experience caused a discontinuity of life. The poet David Jones gave his fictionalised memoir of combat the title of *In Parenthesis* because his experience of war was so apart, so fenced off, from ordinary life.

Every war throughout history has in some way altered the personality and character of some of the men who experienced combat. World War I is different from the others in the persistence and widespread nature of this alteration. The best people to describe the warfare of 1914–18 are probably the soldiers involved, even if they are not necessarily the best qualified to analyse its effects.

I have taken brief extracts from many contemporary letters and diaries to show, overall, the experience of war. That these comments were made in letters and diaries is important because the writers could never have intended their thoughts and observations to be published. They were written for a wife or parent or some other family member. In the case of a diary they were probably only to remind the diarist, at some later date, of his days as a warrior. Each of the extracts reveals something about the unpleasantness, at best, and the vile horror at worst, of the war. Put together they amount to an exposé of what it was that the 'Great Captains' expected men to endure in the name of God, King and Country – and their own egotism. Perhaps they said, 'Who knows, today I might get another decoration!'

In a few cases, the soldier writers of these letters are explicit in their indictment of senior leadership, in many cases the indictment is implicit. In all cases they reveal the truth about the reality of war and the futility of British tactics. The soldiers' testimony against their commanders is damning.

Captain Arthur Adam

9 July 1916. It gives me a fierce feeling of hatred of the present bondage that is hardly to be borne – and there are times on parade when it seems impossible to do what one is told. You begin to sympathise with the socialist who wants to revolt against any and everything.

Captain Adam, of the Cambridgeshire Regiment, joined the Army while still an undergraduate. He was reported wounded and missing on 16 September 1916, at the age of 22. His body was never found.

Captain Garnet Adcock

20 December 1917. Everyone here is 'fed-up' of the war, but not with the Hun. The British staff, British methods, and British bungling have sickened us. We are 'military socialists' and all overseas troops have had enough of the English. How I wish we were with our own people instead of under the English all the time!

Captain Adcock was an officer of the 2nd Australian Tunnelling Company and became a major. He survived the war.

Lieut. John Allen

28 May 1915. I now know that trench life is an unimaginable mixture of horror, strain, discomfort and fineness.

While the trench was being sited, an incident occurred that drove strain out of one's mind to make room for horror. Before I came here and fought in a war, I read casualty lists with sympathy but without intense emotion. But nothing can convey to you how dreadful is the sight of the suffering, badly wounded man – nothing can convey it to you. I heard two short surprised coughs, and saw a man bend and fall. A friend darted to him, opened his tunic, and said to him: 'You're done, Ginger, you're done; they've got you.' This frankness really seemed the most appropriate and sincere thing. They bandaged him up, with the lint every soldier carries inside his tunic; then, knowing evidently that I had a medicine chest with sedatives, he asked for me. By a stroke of providence I was given a beautiful pocket-case with gelatine lamels of a number of drugs. It cost twenty-seven shillings – and under present circumstances worth ten times the money. By the light of the moon – useful for once – I read and tore off the perforated strip. While I was with him he said some remarkable things. I had only known him a day or so, but spotted him at once as a first-rate soldier. He said, 'Shall I go to heaven or hell, sir?' I said with perfect confidence: 'To heaven.' He said: 'No, tell me as a man.' I repeated what I had said. He said: 'At any rate I'll say my prayers,' and I heard him murmuring the common meal grace. A little later he made up a quite beautiful prayer – 'Oh, God, be good and ease my pain – if only a little;' and then: 'I thought I knew what pain was.' All the while it was unbearable to see what he suffered. Someone digging in the trench hard by said: 'He's sinking.' He said, 'What's that?' I said: 'He means the trench.' And then, slowly drawn out: 'I didn't mean to groan, but' – in a long-drawn-out groan – 'I must.' It was intolerable.

Lieut. Allen, a New Zealander, served with the Worcestershire

Regiment, and was killed at Gallipoli, 6 June 1915, at the age of 28.

Major Francis Anderson

6 November 1916. I now go further still in my opinion of the War. I won't express it on paper, because being a soldier by profession it would not be considered suitable. Your attitude is *wrong* like everybody else's at home, who doesn't realise it. If people would cease to be stupidly casual and untruthful when on leave and let people know the truth, you for one would very soon alter your opinion. You may remember I gave you a pretty shrewd idea about the Somme battle, long before it started.

Major Anderson, of the Royal Horse Artillery and Royal Field Artillery, won the MC and was killed in action in France on 25 August 1918 at the age of 23.

Major Sidney Baker

Early 1916. At that moment my servant was hit, and badly too, in the right breast. The crater was partly full of water, and still worse, it was a crater near or in a ditch. These craters are so many bogs and you can imagine what happened. 'Sir, give me a drink. Oh, Sir, do get my legs out!' He was slowly sliding down the crater, with his legs buried and doubling underneath him. I hauled the poor chap to the edge of the crater. He stuck it well but it must have been horrible. I got poor old Barnbrooke up and carried him a few yards; more was impossible, the mud is so horrible. We had started off that afternoon at 3, and now it was past midnight.

[Baker finally dragged his servant to safety.]

The very next night I found myself trying to comfort a wretched wounded man till the stretcher-bearers could get him back to the Aid Post. Poor fellow, I found him there by his cries. He had been calling, calling, calling, hour after hour, ever since a shell had hit him in the darkness, long before dawn, and now it was night again. Poor chap, I doubt if he comes through. It is a horrible business, enough to make a strong man weep. It seems to me just one long degradation.

Major Baker, Gloucestershire Regiment, a schoolmaster, was killed in action, France, 23 March 1918, at the age of 38.

Lieut. W.G. Barlow
2 March 1917. This is an awful war alright. Now I know what it is really. You people at home are spared a dreadful thing and I'd fight again to keep it out of our country. I hope the war will soon stop now as it is sapping out the best of men and all that is beautiful in civilised life.

Lieut. Barlow, of the 58th Australian battalion, was killed in action on 12 May 1917.

Lieut. Denis Barnett
New Year's Eve, 1914. You probably don't know what a village looks like when it has caught it in the neck. Each house has chosen its own way of sitting down, and the whole place is all huge pits where the big high-explosive contact shells have burst. It's an extraordinary experience marching through a place like this for the first time, at night. Perhaps you don't know the two sorts of shells, which are absolutely different. There's the big brute, full of lyddite or melinite or some high explosive, which bursts when it hits the ground, and makes a big hole, blowing out in every direction, but chiefly upwards; so that if you are lying down you are all right, unless the thing bursts on you. This chap does not have any bullets in him, but he does his business in big jaggy bits, which you hear flying around – bzzz, and may kill you some hundreds of yards off, if you are exceptionally unlucky, by dropping on your top-crust. He is generally a heavy shell, fired from a howitzer, and goes dead slow. A Black Maria comes trundling along, whistling in a meditative sort of way, and you can hear her at least four seconds before she gets you.

The other sort is really much more dangerous, as it is full of bullets, and is timed to burst in the air, when the bullets carry on forwards and downwards in a fan shape. He is almost always an express, and comes up not unlike an express train, only faster. The crescendo effect is rather terrifying, but if you are in a trench, and can keep your head down, he can't get at you seriously. The Germans have a little motor battery of 3- inch guns (they gave me my first taste of shrapnel) which is very unpleasant. The shells come in with a mad and ferocious squeal, and burst with a vehemence that is extraordinary for their small size. They have very small bullets in them, and lots of them.

Lieut. Barnett, of the Leinster Regiment, joined the Army on leaving school. He was killed in action, Flanders, 15 August 1915, at the age of 20.

Sergeant A.A. Barwick

24 July 1917. All day long the ground rocked and swayed backwards and forwards from the concussion. Men were driven stark staring mad and more than one of them rushed out of the trench over towards the Germans, any amount of them could be seen crying and sobbing like children their nerves completely gone . . . we were nearly in a state of silliness and half dazed but still the Australians refused to give ground. Men were buried by the dozen, but were frantically dug out again some dead and some alive.

Sergeant Barwick served with the Australian 1st Battalion and survived the war.

Sergeant T. Berry

Winter 1917. We heard screaming coming from a crater a bit away. I went over to investigate it with a couple of the lads. It was a big hole and there was a fellow of the 8th Suffolks in it up to his shoulders. So I said, 'Get your rifles, one man in the middle to stretch them out, make a chain and let him get hold of it.' But it was no use. It was too far to stretch, we couldn't get any force on it, and the more he struggled the further he seemed to go down. He kept begging us to shoot him. But we couldn't shoot him. Who could shoot him? We stayed with him, watching him go down in the mud. And he died. There must have been thousands up there who died in the mud.

Sergeant Berry served in The Rifle Brigade, won the DCM and survived the war.

Lieut. Henry Butters

22 March 1916. I read between the lines the dangerous fact that you

are thinking a little too much about some of the disgusting details of life at the Front. Now, then, forget it! I, who am over here for the good of my soul and the greater success of the Allied armies, have got to go through a number of extremely unpleasant experiences and become thoroughly familiar with all the sides that go to make up the 'Romance of War'.

Lieut. Butters, an American citizen from a wealthy family, joined the British Army-Royal Field Artillery – in 1915. He was killed in action, France, 31 August 1916, at the age of 24.

Lieut. Hugh Butterworth

Early August 1915. We're out temporarily but shall probably be back tomorrow night. We had an awful time. The whole show lasted about 96 hours and is probably by no means over yet. We may quite easily be shoved into the attack almost at once. This letter fails hopelessly. I can't express what we felt or give you a real idea what Hell looks like. We lost two hundred and fifty men.

Lieut. Butterworth, a schoolmaster at Wanganui, New Zealand, joined the British Army's Rifle Brigade. He was killed in action, Flanders, 25 September 1915, at the age of 30.

Captain Ivar Campbell

France, 1915. Here is the scene I shall remember always: A misty summer morning – I went along a sap-head running towards the German line at right-angles to our own. Looking out over the country, flat and uninteresting in peace, I beheld what at first would seem to be a land ploughed by the ploughs of giants. In England you read of concealed trenches – here we don't trouble about that. Trenches rise up, grey clay, three or four feet above the ground. Save for one or two men – snipers – at the sap- head, the country was deserted. No sign of humanity – a dead land. And yet thousands of men were there, like rabbits concealed. The artillery was quiet; there was no sound but a cuckoo in a shell-torn poplar. Then, as a rabbit in the early morning comes out to crop grass, a German stepped over the enemy trench – the only living thing in sight. 'I'll take him,' says the man near me. And like a rabbit the German falls. And again complete silence and desolation.

Campbell

France 1915. The splutter of shrapnel, the red squeal of field guns, N.E.; the growl of the heavies moving slowly through the air, the cr-r-r-r-ump of their explosion. But in a bombardment all tones mingle and their voice is like machinery running not smoothly but roughly, pantingly, angrily, wildly making shows of peace and wholeness.

You perceive, too, in imagination, men infinitely small, running affrighted rabbits, from the upheaval of the shells, nerve-racked, deafened; clinging to earth, hiding eyes, whispering 'O God, O God!' You perceive, too, other men, sweaty, brown, infinitely small also, moving guns, feeding the belching monster, grimly, quietly pleased.

But with eyes looking over this land of innumerable eruptions, you see no line. The land is inhuman.

But thousands of men are there; men who are below ground, men who have little bodies but immense brains. And the men facing West are saying, 'This is an attack, they will attack when this hell's over,' and they go on saying this to themselves continually.

And the men facing East are saying, 'We have got to get over the parapet. We have got to get over the parapet – when the guns lift.'

And then the guns lift up their heads and so a long, higher song.

And then untenanted land is suddenly alive with little men, rushing, stumbling – rather foolishly leaping forward – laughing, shouting, crying in the charge. . ..

There is one thing cheering. The men of the battalion – through all and in spite of that noisy, untasty day; through the wet cold night, hungry and tired, living now in mud and water, with every prospect of more rain to- morrow – are cheery.

Yet under heavy shell-fire it was curious to look into their eyes – some of them little fellows from shops, civilians before, now and after; you perceived the wide, rather frightened, piteous wonder in their eyes, the patient look turned towards you, not, 'What the blankety, blankety hell *is* this?' But 'Is this quite fair?

We cannot move, we are all little animals. Is it quite necessary to make such infernally large explosive shells to kill such infernally small and feeble animals as ourselves?'

Captain Campbell, of the Argyll and Sutherland Highlanders, wrote the two letters shown here in France. He was sent to Mesopotamia, where he was killed in action, 8 January 1916, at the age of 25.

Lieut. Christian Carver

Late July 1916. We got to our gun position and the ordered confusion of getting into action was at its height when with a shriek and a crash a shell burst some yards behind us. Then a bang – and the yell of the shell case as it went through us. I remember looking down the battery. The driver standing beside me was lying killed. A gunner who was behind me got the shrapnel ball I should otherwise have had, in the stomach. Someone was bending over Wager and I saw Norman crawling into the trench with his legs broken. Wounded men lying about, some dead horses.

Carver

14 March 1917. We are in sight of getting out of this hideous bit of country over which the worst fighting has passed. Perhaps you imagine it as a place of broken trees and ruined houses. As a fact there is nothing – Nothing. We live in that desolate belt, extending from the Ancre to the Somme, some five miles in depth, where no trees remain to make a show of green in the coming spring and the chateaux and churches are pounded to mounds of red and white dust.

Lieut. Carver, a pupil at Rugby, joined the army from school. While serving with the Royal Field Artillery, he died of wounds, 23 July 1917, at the age of 20.

Lance Corporal Harold Chapin

4 May 1915. This is a week of sensations but I really think last night will be unbeaten at the end of the war. I had taken three men in answer to a message incoherently delivered by a man on horseback, accompanied by two cyclists. 'Man gone mad. They have got 'im in a little room – by the railway station.'

We found him not raving but apparently asleep, wrapped in blankets, quiet as death. A stretcher was brought out of the motor and about a dozen spare stretcher slings I had thought to bring – fortunately – and we debated a moment in the moonlight. What a curious group we must have been on the deserted station platform, standing round him! Then one of his chums touched him. You must imagine more than I can describe in this chatter. He raved and bit and beat out with fists and feet snarling like a dog – *really* like a dog – we got him on to a stretcher, and I lashed him on as gently as I could but very firmly. Once bending across him I touched his face with my sleeve, he had it in his teeth in a minute – and in the midst of it men passed going up to the trenches singing. They passed along the road not 50 yards away while a dozen of us held him down by arms and legs and hair, and muffled him in blankets and packed him off with two of our men and two of his chums to our snug little brand new hospital. Ashcroft and I then set out to walk back to our station.

Chapin
29 May 1915. If you at home could only see and hear the enormous concentration of force necessary to take a mile of German trench; the terrific resistance we have to put up to hold it; the price we have to pay over every little failure – a price paid with no purchase to show for it.

Lance Corporal Chapin, an American, was an actor, producer and dramatist before he joined the Royal Army Medical Corps. He was killed in action, France, 26 September 1915, at the age of 29.

Second Lieut. William Dyson
21 May 1916. It's one thing to lead fresh troops into battle in the beginning of the day. It's another thing to go up at nightfall with the vague consciousness that the game is up. The aftermath of any battle is tragic. The aftermath of an apparent failure is more so than usual. It was with strange feelings that the little party of NCOs and men marched up to the firing line that night. Attempts at facetiousness fell flat. The continuous roar of guns and bursting of black and woolly shrapnel over the villages kept bringing us

back to the situation before us. The last village we passed through was dimly illuminated by the lurid glare of burning houses in the main street. We reported to Brigade Headquarters and were straightway despatched to our own. An officer who had returned after fourteen hours in a shell hole asked if I would get 2 men and a stretcher and follow him into 'No-Man's-Land'. One jumped at something to do and followed on through the old communication trenches we had learned to know so well. Then out over the parapet, over the endless maze of trenches straggling to and from the front line, stumbling about amongst the shell holes and barbed wire illuminated from time to time by the more brilliant of the German flares. At last we reached the front line, straggled over it with the stretcher and trundled on into 'No-Man's-Land'. I was warned to have a revolver handy. Quite why one didn't know, for the rifles of both sides were at rest. Only the artillery men had the energy to carry on the noisy game, and the Germans, fearing another attack, kept putting up continuous flares. I shall never forget that night. The strangest I have ever spent. We had only two stretchers with us and were trying to find two men we knew to be particularly bad. It was impossible to find them in the dark and we just took the men who seemed to need us most and returned. It's no light task carrying a man over ground like that. We all took turns but it seemed appallingly slow. We had just reached the most difficult point in the journey where our wire had been most blown about by the bombardment when the bosche artillery decided to put what is known as a minor barrage on that part of the line. Three times I tried to find a way through the wire without success. The only thing to do was to try and get him down into the trench which was already full of wounded going down. After an unconscionable time we managed to get him down to the aid post. The men were absolutely done so we handed over the stretcher to proper stretcher bearers and returned to the Company. It seemed almost hopeless.

Lieut. Dyson, of the 16th London Regiment, had been a candidate for the Wesleyan Ministry. He died of wounds while a prisoner of war, France, 26 July 1916.

Private Thomas Dry

15 January 1916. Imagine you are all sitting down to a meal with

friends around you, when all of a sudden by some unseen hand the person to whom you are speaking drops dead by your side. Before you have recovered a head flies off another of your friends, and you then look around, and seeing nothing, you gaze on what is before you.

Private Dry, of the 23rd Battalion, AIF, had been a watchmaker. He was killed in action, France, 4 August 1916, at the age of 28.

Sergeant L.R. Elvin

25 July 1916. Heavy firing all morning – simply murder. Men falling everywhere. . . . Expecting death every second. 23 men smothered in one trench. Dead and dying everywhere. Some simply blown to pieces. Shells falling like hail during a storm. Five left in trench.

Sergeant Elvin, of the Australian 1st Battalion, was killed in action on 5 May 1917.

Colonel Rowland Feilding

20 February 1917. My God! If the people at home could actually see with their eyes this massacring of the cream of our race, what a horrible shock it would be to them.

Feilding

8 October 1917. The section of the front line which I hold is more or less of a graveyard. Many soldiers lie buried in the parapet and in some cases their feet project into the trench. We come across others as we dig. If you saw it all you wouldn't know whether to laugh or cry.

Feilding

November 1917. Spit and polish is the order of the day and I am all for it – in reason. But when the men have just come out, after sixteen days in the line, where they have been squeezed up in muddy dugouts during the few hours in the daytime when they were not on duty and could get a sleep – for they stand to all night – I think it is a bit thick when high-placed officers, who do not share the dangers and discomforts, and indeed never or scarcely ever, go into the firing line, kick up Hell's delight because the bayonet scabbards are not polished. Yet such is the kind of thing we have sometimes to put up with from our friends behind the front. Personally, I prefer the attentions of our enemies. These are at least logical, and so think all the front line. Although, during the sixteen days and nights the battalion has been up, the breastworks have been collapsed by the rains – to say nothing of German shells and trench mortars; though our patrols have nightly explored No-Man's-Land and the German wire, not a word is said about that. Not a remark. Not a comment. It is *polished* bayonet scabbards that they want. Can you believe it?

Colonel Feilding was appointed captain in the Coldstream Guards in 1915. In 1916 he was given command, as a lieut.-colonel, of the 6th Battalion Connaught Rangers and later of the 1st Civil Service Rifles. He won the DSO, little enough for the length and quality of his unbroken front line service. He survived the war.

Lieut. Graham Greenwell

17 August 1916. You wouldn't be able to conceive the filthy and miserable surroundings in which I am writing this note – not even if you were accustomed to the filthiest slums of Europe. I am sitting in the bottom of an old German dugout about ten or twelve feet under the earth with three other officers and about ten men; the table is littered with food, candle grease and odds and ends. The floor is covered with German clothing and filth. The remains of the trench outside is blown to pieces and full of corpses from the different regiments which have been here lately, German and English. The stench is well nigh intolerable. Everybody is absolutely worn out with fatigue and hunger. I wandered on around these awful remains of trenches, simply sickened by the sights and smells, until I found some poor devils cowering in the filth, where they had been for forty-eight hours. I shall never look on warfare either as fine or sporting again. It reduces men to shivering beasts.

Lieut. Greenwell was commissioned into the 4th Battalion Oxfordshire and Buckinghamshire Light Infantry at the age of 18. He won the MC and survived the war.

Sergeant-Major Frederic Keeling

23 December 1915. *The Chronicle* published some time ago some rot from some blithering correspondent who, I suppose drives about comfortably in GHQ motor-cars and thinks it a wonderful thing to come under shell fire, to the effect that all the troops are comfortably housed for the winter in nice warm huts. That sort of thing makes men sweat out here. I don't grumble at a tent with a coke fire (when coke is available) even in the coldest weather; but it is a bloody shame to deceive the public at home and say we are in comfortable huts when we aren't. Till the autumn we hadn't even got tents, but generally just our waterproof sheets as roofs for bivvy shelters.

In our brigade a man is damned lucky if he gets a dozen hours' sleep in three days in the trenches – it's working and carrying parties whenever it isn't sentry and listening post, and trench mortars and whizz-bangs on and off all day and night in the intervals of bombardments. I don't pretend to have been through anything like as much as men who have been out here eight months and never missed the trenches, but I have been through enough to know what they have been through. And then people think it is mud and wet we mind; that is nothing, absolutely nothing, compared with the nerve-racking hell of bombardment. Of course, people at home can imagine that more easily than the bombardments, so that is what they talk about. I can't think that human nature ever had to stand in any kind of warfare in history what the modern infantryman has to stand.

Sergeant-Major Keeling, of Duke of Cornwall's Light Infantry, was a writer and student on economic and social affairs. He was killed in action, France, 18 August 1916, at the age of 30.

Captain Thomas Kettle

8 September 1916. If I live I mean to spend the rest of my life working for perpetual peace. I have seen war and faced modern artillery and I know what an outrage it is against simple men. We are moving tonight into the battle of the Somme. The bombardment, destruction and bloodshed are beyond all imagination. The big guns are coughing and smacking their shells, which sound for

all the world like overhead express trains, at anything from 10 to 100 per minute on this sector.

Captain Kettle served in Royal Dublin Fusiliers. He had been a barrister, a member of parliament and Professor of National Economics, National University, Dublin. He was killed in action, France, 9 September 1916, at the age of 32.

Sister E.E. Luard

22 May 1916. They [her soldier patients] are all being angels of patience and silence, only asking for things, even drinks, when they are absolutely obliged. One who died today said yesterday that he had 'nothing to complain about', and was afraid he was a great trouble! We've had three officers in – one nearly died when he was having his foot taken off. One who had his arm blown off was laid in a dugout and that was blown in on him and it took two hours to dig him out. Another one was buried for 15 hours. He died this evening. A boy who was trephined [a skull operation] and has one eye destroyed and the other covered up, never speaks, but kicks off every stitch of clothing and breaks out into, 'Lead, Kindly Light' and 'God Save the King'. . . . The big ward with beds all round and two lines down the middle is a very sad place – quite full of wrecks – and not one of them ever well enough even to speak to any other one. The next acute hut with beds is also very busy with compound fractures, heads and amputations, and some chests. But the worst chests, and the abdominals and the bombed people with several serious wounds, are in the big ward. A whole line of our front trench has been buried with men in it, under thousands and thousands of shells bursting at once dead on it.

Sister Luard, who was awarded the Royal Red Cross, served in France for almost the entire war.

Sergeant L.J. Martin

31 July 1916. There were dead and wounded everywhere. . . . I had to sit on top of a dead man as there was no picking and choosing . . . I saw a shell lob about twelve yards away and it lifted two men right up in the air for about six feet and they

simply dropped back dead. One or two of the chaps got shell shock and others got really frightened it was piteous to see them . . . One great big chap got away as soon as he reached the firing line and could not be found. I saw him in the morning in a dug out he was white with fear and shaking like a leaf. One of our Lieuts. got shell shock and he literally cried like a child, some that I saw carried down out of the firing line were struggling and calling out for their mother, while others were blabbering sentences one could not make out. A badly wounded chap had his body partly in a small hole that had a good deal of wood work about it, this somehow got alight and all I could see was the lower parts of his legs and a piece of his face, all the rest was burned.

Sergeant Martin, of the 1st Australian Machine-Gun Battalion, survived the war.

Captain William Mason
Autumn 1915. The suffering of the men at the Front, of the wounded whose flesh and bodies are torn in a way you cannot conceive.

Captain Mason, a lecturer at Bristol University, served with the Gloucestershire Regiment. He was killed in action, France, 3 July 1916, at the age of 27.

Captain G.D. Mitchell MC, DCM
2 June 1916. I feel disaster in my blood. Curse all the powers that bungled us to defeat. My thoughts were bitter as I looked down at my service stripes. What if they were all for nothing.

Captain Mitchell, of the 48th Australian battalion, won the MC and DCM and survived the war.

Private E.O. Neaves
15 February 1917. All my pals I came over with are gone, but 7 out of 150 remain, it's simply scientific murder, not war at all. As for seeing Germans it's all lies you never get close enough to do that, unless in a charge, I keep smiling, but I tell you it takes some doing. The premonition I had when leaving Sydney, that I would never see home again still hangs about me – one would be

unnatural to go through uninjured, if I get out of it with a leg and arm off I'll be perfectly satisfied, so you will understand what it is like. Don't get married till after the war.

Private Neave's premonition was fulfilled. He was killed in action on 6 November 1917, at the age of 25, while serving with the 20th Battalion.

Sergeant Ernest Nottingham

27 March 1916. I spoke of the hardening of experience. Here's an instance. I've just come from where fifty thousand bodies lie, bones and barbed wire everywhere, skeletons bleached if one takes a walk over the frightfully contested and blown up hill. Boots and bones protruding from one's dugout walls.

Sergeant Nottingham enlisted at the age of 38 in the 15th London Regiment, won the DCM and died of wounds on 7 June 1917.

Corporal James Parr

20 March 1916. Oh! This Army! At times I feel I could scream and put straws in my hair; and I probably should if I didn't laugh. We are so messed about and badgered from pillar to post that I hardly know which way to turn.

Corporal Parr, 16th London Regiment, was reported wounded and missing, France, 1 July 1916, at the age of 27.

Lieut. Robert Pickering

1 September 1915. The trenches we had held were lost in a famous flammerwerfer attack and are now untenable to either side. They are now only occupied by the heaps of dead men who lost them. To our left some of the lost ground was regained and further trenches taken but immediately to our left through the wood is a ridge untenable to either side – it is simply ploughed up with thousands of shell craters – a great mine crater and thousands of dead. The undergrowth of this wood is very thick and the Huns could creep right up to our trench to throw bombs or surprise us. To provide against that we have a screen of listening patrols and bombers concealed in the scrub, they patrol our old

trenches and the untenanted ridge – the Hun patrols do the same
– directly any alarm is given the bombers lie down and join the
huge army of stinking unburied dead. Rats by the thousands get
food here – they go into a man at one place, they come out at
another – the shrubs are littered with dead men and the rats
which feed on them often make a noise and cause alarm. Both
sides have been piling up guns and strengthening their artillery in
this locality for 10 months. Nearly all recent attacks on both sides
have been here at the tip of the salient and all the guns are trained
on it. The shell fire never ceases and at intervals regular bombardments take place for hours on end – to put the wind up the
other party. This morning early we were in an absolute inferno
for a long time and we get that kind of thing about every other
day. You get perhaps 5/700 guns going on both sides together,
and the number of shells of calibres that come over are numbered
in tens of thousands. It's remarkable how one can live through
such an inferno. It nearly drives you mad. Conditions are getting
worse and worse for the poor infantry who man the trenches – it is
simply an artillery duel.

For God's sake don't conjure up visions of our old happy days
to me, old man – it seems wicked to think of such things when
perhaps 10,000 or more men have been killed in this wretched
hole within a square mile in the last four months – these woods
were lovely once – now the trees are all bare and strafed and
blackened, they lie broken against one another, they lie on dead
men squashing them. If the dead are buried at all they are buried
in tens, twenties, hundreds together – they are lucky to be buried
at all.

Love and good luck old chap to yourself and don't go asking for
trouble. Keep your head if you can and if you are in trenches no
matter how heavily they are shelled – don't leave them for the
open behind. I've seen a battalion almost wiped out through
leaving their trenches like that. The Germans send over a curtain
of shrapnel like hail at once and you have no chance.

Lieut. Pickering, a bank of New South Wales employee,
enlisted in the Royal Field Artillery. He was killed in action,
France, 30 November 1917, at the age of 25.

Lieut. Adrian Stephen

July 1916. I met an Infantry officer. He was grey in the face.

'Well,' he said, 'what do you think of it?'

'Seems all right.'

'Um, we got to their third line and were driven back. We are barely holding our own front line. We're – we're – wiped out. The General's a broken man.'

'But Gommecourt?'

'Lost.'

'Another Loos,' I said.

'Looks it.' He turned away.

I felt tired suddenly. The few yards home were miles. The world was full of stretchers and white faces, and fools who gibbered about the great advance.

Lieut. Stephen, who was educated at Sydney University, New South Wales, was killed in action, Flanders, 14 March 1918.

Corporal A.G. Thomas

25 July 1916. For Christ's sake write a book on the life of an infantryman, and by so doing you will quickly prevent these shocking tragedies.

Thomas

3 August 1916. I am loaded like a pack horse carrying twelve bombs, 250 rounds of ammunition, haversack, coat, two gas helmets, rifle. I have seen things here that will make the bloody military aristocrats' name stink for ever. The soldiers I pity as they have been ruled into this farce. God, it is cruel. What humans will stand is astounding. Tonight will be another long vigil gazing into death, this is truly the Valley of the Shadow. God the whole chaos is too terrific for my pencil.

Corporal Thomas was a member of the Australian 6th Battalion, he was killed in action on 8 June 1918.

Sergeant A.L. de Vine

8 August 1915. The stench of the dead bodies now is simply awful as they have been exposed to the sun for several days, many have swollen terribly and have burst.

Sergeant de Vine served in the AIF 4th Battalion and survived the war. He wrote this diary entry at Gallipoli.

Lieut. J.S. Williams
3 October 1915. My dugout in the trench had other occupants, things with lots of legs, also swarms of rats and mice. I think I have slept in every conceivable place of filth. I did not have my clothes off for the whole time I was in the trenches and it rained the whole time.

Lieut. Williams, a Canadian, survived the war.

Captain Theodore Wilson
1 June 1916. We had to collect what had been a man the other day and put it into a sandbag and bury it, and less than two minutes before he had been laughing and talking and *thinking*.

Captain Wilson of the Sherwood Foresters, was a schoolmaster and writer. He was killed in action, France, 23 March 1918, at the age of 29.

Private A.J. Wood
November 1917. Grieve for me not, my darling, but for our homeland. When one knows all that our Boys have gone through, the conditions that they are living under, and the unconquerable spirit which enables them to make light of their trials and dangerous undertakings, one's heart aches to think of the inestimable loss to the Nation of all those precious lives.

Private Wood, of the AIF, was killed in action, France, 6 November 1917, at the age of 34.

SELECT
BIBLIOGRAPHY
and SOURCES

Of the vast array of books concerning World War I, I list only those which I found most helpful. In addition, other books are mentioned under Notes at the end of each chapter. Many thousands of documents are available for reading at the Imperial War Museum, London, Public Records Office, Kew and Chancery Lane, both in London, Liddell Hart Centre for Military Archives of King's College, London, the National Library of Scotland, Edinburgh and the Australian War Memorial, Canberra. Much other material about World War I is to be found in various issues of the *Journal* of the Royal United Services Institution and *The Army Quarterly*. I have drawn on veterans' letters in my own archives and on interviews and conversations with many veterans. When I was a young soldier during World War II, I was often in the company of men who had fought during the earlier conflict and had rejoined the army for another war. Their recollections of events, then only 20 years behind them and still vivid, were invaluable.

Arthur, Sir George. *Lord Haig*, Heinemann, 1928.
Aspinall-Oglander, Brigadier-General C.F. *Military Operations, Gallipoli*, 2 vols. Heinemann, 1929.
Babington, Antony. *For the Sake of Example: Capital Courts*

Martial 1914–18, Leo Cooper, 1983.

Baldwin, Hanson. *World War I: An Outline History*, Hutchinson, 1963.

Barker, A.J. *Townshend of Kut*, Cassell, 1967.

Barrie, Alexander. *War Underground*, Muller, 1962.

Baynes, John. *Morale: A Study of Men and Courage*, Leo Cooper, 1987.

Bean, C.E.W. *The Australian Official Histories*, Angus & Robertson, Sydney. Vols I & II *The AIF at Gallipoli*, published 1937; Vol III *The AIF in France in 1916*, published 1929; Vol IV *The AIF in France in 1917*, published 1933; Vol V *The AIF in France in 1918*, published 1943; Vol VI, *The AIF in France in 1918*, published 1942.

Behrand, Arthur. *As From Kemmel Hill*, Eyre & Spottiswoode, 1963.

Behrand, Arthur. *Make Me a Soldier: A Platoon Commander in Gallipoli*, Eyre & Spottiswoode, 1961.

Blake, Robert. (ed.) *The Private Papers of Douglas Haig*, Eyre & Spottiswoode, 1952.

Boraston, J.H. *Sir Douglas Haig's Despatches*, Dent, 1919.

Callwell, Major-General C.E. *The Dardanelles*, Constable, 1924.

Cameron, James. *1914*, Cassell, 1959.

Carew, Tim. *The Vanished Army: The British Expeditionary Force 1914–1915*, Kimber, 1964.

Caesar, George H. *Kitchener: Architect of Victory*, William Kimber, 1977.

Chapman, Guy. (ed.) *Vain Glory*, Cassell, 1937.

Charteris, Brigadier-General John. *Field Marshal Earl Haig*, London, 1929.

Churchill, Winston. *The World Crisis 1911–1918*, 2 vols, Odhams, 1923.

Cooper, Duff. *Haig*, 2 vols, Faber, 1935.

Coppard, George. *With a Machine Gun to Cambrai*, HMSO, 1969.

Cutlack, F.W. *War Letters of General Monash*, Angus & Robertson, 1935.

Davidson, Major-General Sir John. *Haig – Master of the Field*,

Peter Nevill, 1953.

Dewar, G.A.B. & Lt.-Col. Boraston. *Sir Douglas Haig's Command 1915–1918*, Constable, 1922.

Dixon, Norman F. *On the Psychology of Military Incompetence*, Cape, 1976.

Dolden, A. Stuart. *Cannon Fodder*, Blandford Press, Poole, 1980.

Dunn, Captain J.C. *The War the Infantry Knew 1914–1919*, Jane's, 1987.

Edmonds, Charles, (real name, Charles Carrington) *A Subaltern's War*, Peter Davies, 1930.

Edmonds, Brigadier-General Sir James. *Military Operations*, The British Official History. Numerous volumes published between 1922 and 1938.

Ellis, John. *Eye-Deep in Hell: Trench Warfare in World War I*, Croom Helm, 1976.

—— ? *Eye-Witnesses's Narrative of the War: From the Marne to Neuve Chapelle, September 1914–March 1915*, Edward Arnold, 1915.

Farrar-Hockley, Anthony. *Death of an Army: The First Battle of Ypres*, Arthur Barker, 1967.

Feilding, Rowland. *War Letters to a Wife*, Medici, London, 1929.

Ferro, Marc. *The Great War 1914–1918*, Routledge, 1969.

Fuller, Major-General J.F.C. *The Conduct of War 1789–1961*, Eyre & Spottiswoode, 1961.

Fussell, Paul. *The Great War and Modern Memory*, Oxford University Press, 1975.

Gammage, Bill. *The Broken Years: Australian Soldiers in the Great War*, Penguin, 1975.

Gardner, R.B. *The Big Push: A Portrait of the Battle of the Somme*, Cassell, 1961.

Gibbons, S.R. and Morican, P. *World War One*, Longman, 1965.

Gilbert, Martin. *First World War Atlas*, Weidenfeld & Nicolson, 1970.

Gough, General Sir Hubert. *The Fifth Army*, London, 1931.

Groom, W.H.A. *Poor Bloody Infantry: The Truth Untold*, Picardy, London, 1983. 'G.S.O.' *G.H.Q. (Montreuil)*, Philip Allan, London, 1920.

Haig, The Countess. *The Man I Knew: The Intimate Life-Story of Douglas Haig*, The Moray Press, London, 1936.

Haig, Major-General Douglas. *Cavalry Studies, Strategical and Tactical*, London, 1907.

Haking, Brigadier-General R.C.B. *Company Training*, London, 1913.

Hamilton, General Sir Ian. *Gallipoli Diary*, 2 vols, Edward Arnold, 1920.

Hankey, Lord. *The Supreme Command 1914–1918*, 2 vols, Allen & Unwin, 1961.

Harington, General Sir Charles. *Plumer of Messines*, John Muray, 1935.

Harris, John. *The Somme: Death of a Generation*, Zenith, London, 1966.

Hart, B.H. Liddell. *Reputations*, London, 1928.

Hart, B.H. Liddell. *History of the First World War*, Cassell, London, 1970.

Harvey, H.E. *Battle Line Narratives*, Brentano's, London, 1928.

Herwig, Holger, H. and Heyman, Neil M. *Biographical Dictionary of World War I*, Greenwood Press, Connecticut, 1982.

Horne, Alistair. *Death of a Generation: Neuve Chapelle to Verdun and the Somme*, Macdonald, 1970.

Houlihan, Michael. *World War I: Trench Warfare*, Ward Lock, London, 1974.

Housman, Lawrence (ed.) *War Letters of Fallen Englishmen*, Gollancz, 1930.

Keegan, John. *The Face of Battle*, London, 1978.

Laffin, John. *Letters from the Front 1914–1918*, Dent, London, 1973.

Laffin, John. *Tommy Atkins: The Story of the British Soldier*, Cassell, 1966.

Laffin, John. *On the Western Front. Soldiers Stories from France and Flanders*, Alan Sutton, Gloucester, 1986.

Laffin, John. *Damn the Dardanelles! The Agony of Gallipoli*, Macmillan, Australia, 1985.

Leed, Eric J. *No Man's Land: Combat & Identity in World War I*, Cambridge University Press, 1979.

SELECT BIBLIOGRAPHY AND SOURCES

Lloyd, Alan. *The War in the Trenches*, Hart-Davis, MacGibbon, 1976.

Marshall-Cornwall, James. *Haig as a Military Commander*, Batsford, 1976.

Martin, Christopher. *Battle of the Somme*, Wayland, London, 1973.

Maxwell, W.M. *A Psychological Retrospect of the Great War*, London, 1923.

McNair, Wilson. *Blood and Iron*, Seeley, Service & Co., 1916.

Moorehead, Alan. *Gallipoli*, Hamish Hamilton, 1956.

Morris, Alan. *Bloody April*, Jarrolds, 1967.

North, John. *Gallipoli, The Fading Vision*, Faber, 1936.

Pitt, Barrie. *1918 The Last Act*, Cassell, 1962.

Pugsley, Christopher. *Gallipoli: The New Zealand Story*, Hodder & Stoughton, 1984.

Robbins, Keith. *The First World War*, Oxford University Press, 1984.

Russell, Arthur. *The Machine Gunner*, Roundwood Press, Kineton, U.K., 1977.

Secrett, Sergeant T. *25 Years with Earl Haig*, London 1930.

Smithers, A.J. *Sir John Monash*, Leo Cooper, 1973.

Swinton, Sir Ernest D. *Over My Shoulder*, Oxford University Press, 1951.

Taylor, A.J.P. *The First World War*, Hamish Hamilton, London, 1963.

Terraine, John. *The Western Front 1914–1918*, London, 1964.

Thompson, P.A. *Lions Led by Donkeys*, Warner Laurie, 1927.

Toland, John. *No Man's Land: The Story of 1918*, Eyre, Methuen, 1980.

Travers, Tim. *The Killing Ground: The British Army, the Western Front and the Emergence of Modern Warfare, 1900–1918*, Allen & Unwin, 1987.

Wade, Aubrey. *The War of the Guns*, Batsford, 1936.

Warner, Philip. *The Battle of Loos*, William Kimber, 1976.

Wilkinson, Frederick. *A Source Book of World War I: Weapons and Uniforms*, Ward Lock, 1979.

Willett, Allen R. and Murray, Williamson, (eds.) *Military Effectiveness: The First World War*, Allen & Unwin, 1988.

Wolff, Leon. *In Flanders' Fields: The 1917 Campaign*, Penguin, 1979.

Woodget, Dudley. *World War I: A Sketchmap History*, Longman, 1976.

Woodward, David. *Lloyd George and the Generals*, Delaware, 1983.

Woodward, Llewellyn. *Great Britain and the War of 1914–1918*, Methuen, 1967.

The pro-Haig school is strongly represented by John Terraine in his various books; the various books of B.H. Liddell Hart provide an antithetical point of view.

Four books stand out as essential reading in terms of modern scholarship and research into World War I. They are: Travers' *The Killing Ground: The British Army, the Western Front and the Emergence of Modern Warfare, 1900–1918*: Leed's *No Man's Land: Combat and Identity in World War I*: Fussell's *The Great War and Modern Memory*: and Gilbert's *First World War Atlas*.

INDEX

INDEX

INDEX

INDEX

INDEX